GOOD PUP
GOOD DOG

GOOD PUP GOOD DOG

Su Harvey

First published in the UK by Interpet Publishing
Vincent Lane, Dorking, Surrey, RH4 3YX

ISBN 978-1-84286-142-4

Reproduction by Universal Graphics PTE LTD, Singapore

Printed by Vychodoslovenske Tlaciarne, a.s., Slovakia

Conceived, edited, designed and produced by
Duncan Petersen Publishing Ltd
C7 Old Imperial Laundry, Warriner Gardens,
London, SW11 4XW

Picture credits on page 208

Editor Hermione Edwards

Production editor Jacqui Sayers

Editorial director Andrew Duncan

Designers Ian Midson, Anthony Limerick

Cover design Nigel Soper

Photographer Bill Stephenson

CONTENTS

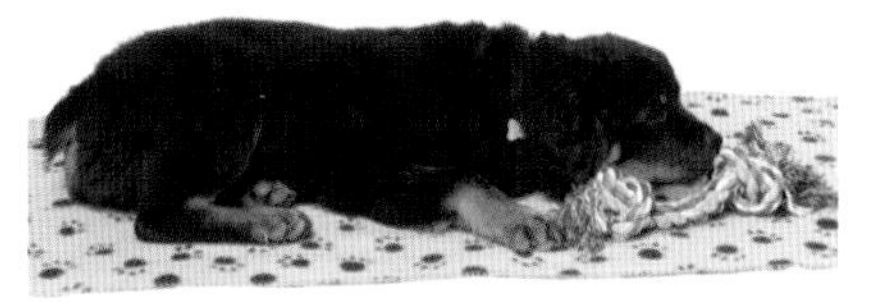

INTRODUCTION

From the day you bring your new puppy or dog home, this book is for you. **Good Pup, Good Dog** will enable you to enjoy a wonderful friendship with a happy and well-trained dog.

Emphasizing your body language in harmony with your natural ability to manage a dog will make educating your puppy or dog easier than you ever realized. Having trained dogs for many, many years I have found that it is not difficult, as long as you give clear signals with your body and face.

Not just this, but some of your signals should show a sense of humour. Dogs *do* have a sense of humour and get great pleasure themselves when you laugh (so laughing when your dog does something wrong is not a good idea).

We love our pets, but sometimes we may not like them because they behave badly. So, even if you have had your dog for some time, this book is still for you. You *can* teach an old dog new tricks, or retrain unruly traits.

Remember, above all, that dog training starts at home. Unless you have control there, you most certainly will not have it elsewhere.

In the end, your aim (and mine in this book) is to have a dog so well trained that if the leash breaks you are still in total control. Or, if you run out of treats and rewards, your dog will still respond to commands.

Su Harvey

Good and bad body language – an introduction

GOOD. The body language here is very welcoming.

GOOD. This body language can be seen clearly from a distance. Used for calling your dog to you.

GOOD. Showing him the position to come to as he approaches – just like parking a car.

GOOD.
Once your dog is sitting in front of you, facing you, he will be ready for the next signal. A clear sign instructing him to trot a circle behind you in order to end up at the heel position, ready to join you for a walk.

GOOD.
Note the stiffness and position of the body. This means 'Keep away: not interested'.

GOOD.
Easily readable as 'Come and play with me'.

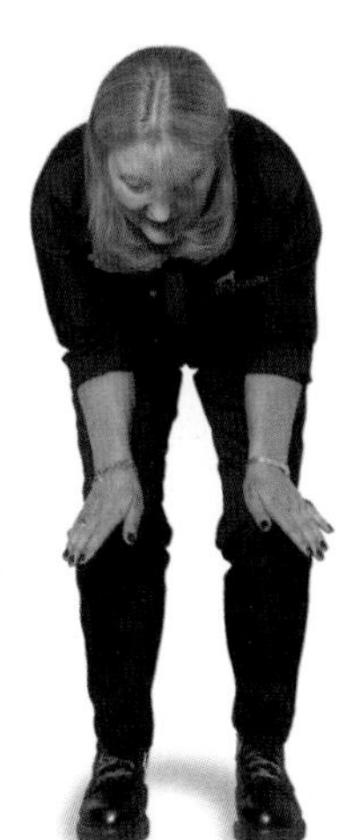

BAD.
Bending over and patting the legs could confuse. All the dog will see is the top of the head.

BAD.
Towering over a dog can be threatening and pushes the dog away.

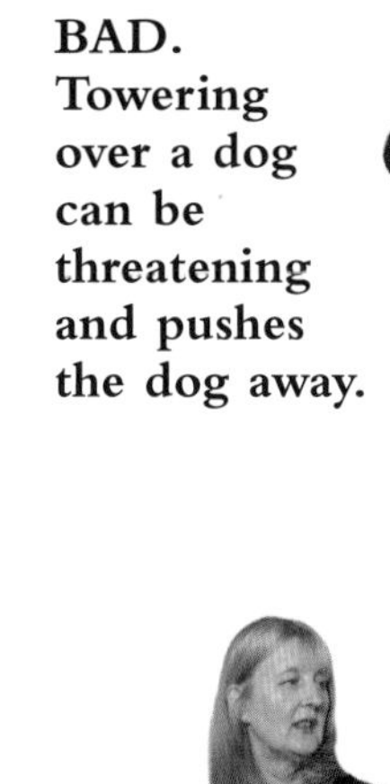

BAD.
This finger deserves to be bitten off.

BAD.
Certainly looks like no interest in playing.

BODY LANGUAGE BASICS

Whenever humans give out body language signals, they use slight variations in posture, as do dogs. Slightly bending forwards is natural, especially with a smaller dog. Try to bend at the knees rather than tower over a dog.

Each handler's body language differs slightly because of their own natural pose. So, while following my guidelines, keep faith with your own instinctive style.

THE THREE FUNDAMENTAL ASSETS

VOICE, FACIAL EXPRESSION AND HAND SIGNALS

It is much easier to train a dog if you understand each other. Your body language will work naturally with your voice, facial expression and hand signals. This is not rocket science – humans use these all the time with each other.

To judge someone's mood without hearing a word is second nature to a dog, just as it is to you. As you get to know your dog and he gets to know you, you will start to read each other's body language without even trying.

Try sitting down on all fours, wag your backside and smile at your partner. Are they laughing? Of course – they realize you're not being serious; you're being playful. What does it mean when a dog does the

What's up with your face?

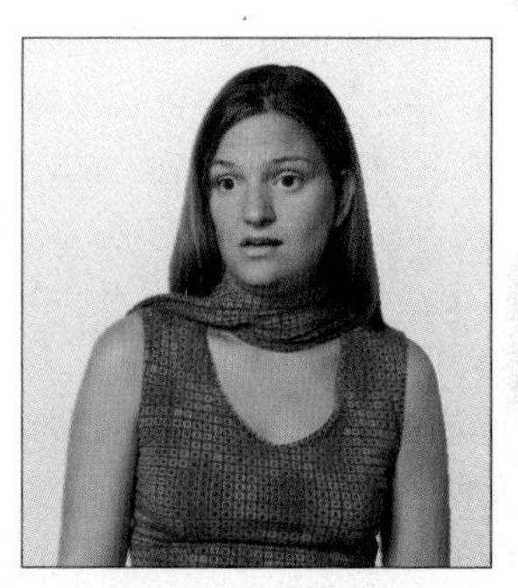

What's that look for?

Who's upset you?

I can see what mood you're in.

same? Play time, of course. Body language awareness really is that easy.

Before you start training a puppy or dog, do some people and dog watching. Try to guess their mood, or what they are expressing.

VOICE

Your first asset is your voice. If you shout, others shout back. So will your dog.

Never shout. This tells your dog that you are not in control, and will confuse him.

DOG VOICES

- The high pitched yap – excitement.
- The growl – warning.
- The deep-throated bark – threatening, warning. Someone's approaching.
- The whine – I'm bored.
- The gentle whine – I'm not well or I'm unhappy.
- The howl – distress signal, call of the wild.
- The yelp – pain (just like the human yelp).

For commands, use a firm, deep, sharp voice. Keep commands short – preferably single words. Not "Will you sit down now? Sit, Sit, Sit", with the voice getting higher and the volume with it. This makes your dog (like you) more and more agitated and frustrated. So, always use the same tone for commands.

HUMAN VOICES

- The deep, sharp voice for commands.
- The higher, calm voice for praise.
- The growl for disapproval.
- The excitable voice for praise and encouragement, or for when you need your dog to move more quickly.
- The whisper to get your dog to focus – this works well in a quiet environment because he will watch your body language all the more closely if he can't quite hear.
- The sharp whisper – look at that.
- The yelp – pain.

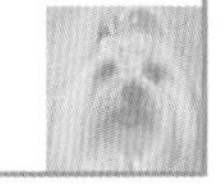

Have confidence that your dog will understand your tone of voice. Gently give a command and follow it up with praise if you see the right response.

PRAISE

Be natural and genuine with your praise: this is a key asset. We can all tell when humans give false praise. So can dogs. If you praise confidently, then your dog will be confident. If you show uncertainty, then your dog will be uncertain. For praise, use a higher tone, but not too

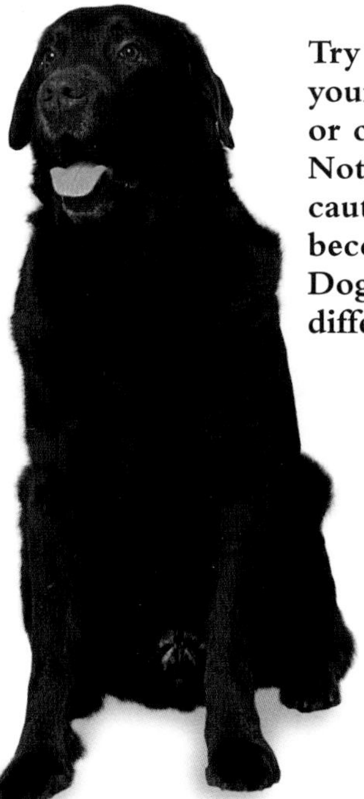

Try this on your partner or children. Note how cautious they become. Dogs are no different.

excitable, otherwise your dog will lose concentration and start to play. To praise a simple exercise such as the sit, a calm tone and "What a good dog" is enough.

If your dog is doing something you don't like, or is not responding to the first command, then use a firmer tone: go deeper, and almost growl. For example, he is about to pick up something smelly and horrible off the ground. Just give a firm, sharp "Leave it", and then praise when he does.

When you call your dog, raise your tone a notch higher and add some excitement. Make your voice welcoming.

FACIAL EXPRESSION

- Smile at your dog when you are pleased.
- Give a dirty look when your dog does something you don't like.
- Scowl for punishment.
- A laughing face says 'It's OK to be excited'.

This book will teach you how to combine voice commands, facial expression and hand signals. When your dog is responding to all three, you will find you can occasionally drop the voice and use hand signals only, or drop the hand signals and use voice and facial expression. Try getting your dog's tail to wag, using one of these assets, then two, then all three.

In the first stage of training,

This says, 'I'm praising you'. Your dog can see instantly that you are pleased. Combine this with a calm, reassuring voice: "Good boy".

This says 'I'm not pleased'. Everyone has different facial expressions, but your dog will soon understand yours, as long as you use them consistently.

This is a little fiercer – a scowl for strongest disapproval.

This should create a very happy dog, especially if you combine it with a high-pitched voice. It's the 'Let's play' signal, and you don't have to get on all fours to get the message across.

while you are developing a relationship with your dog and he is beginning to understand you, some extra motivation is often needed to help with his concentration. This is where treats and toys really come into their own.

Treats are too often used excessively and, once understanding is established, you can cut down on treats and instead play more at the end of the exercises. Play is far more beneficial than treats because it makes you interact with your dog. At the end of an exercise your dog looks at your body language for signs that you are reaching for a treat. Keep your handkerchief in a different pocket – otherwise he'll get excited each time you need to blow your nose.

HAND SIGNALS

See the photographs opposite for the basic hand signal commands. It is essential to master these basic hand signals before you start to train your dog as they are used throughout all of the aspects of training. You should have a calm, still body for the stay. To give excitable praise you should jump about. Turn away from your dog with your arms folded to show disapproval.

All of these tips should be used together with the advice and training exercises that follow in the rest of this book. Remember that you and your dog are working as a team: in a team there has to be a leader, and the two-legged one is best.

Hand signal for the stay.

Hand signal for the sit.

Hand signal for the stand.

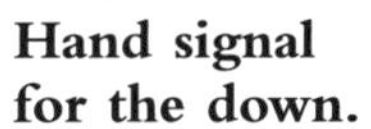

Hand signal for the down.

Hand signal for the leave.

THE NEW ADDITION

PREPARATION

You are going to need:

A stock of food. Find out what your puppy or dog is used to from the previous owner. If you intend to change his food, then do it gradually. If done quickly this could cause an upset stomach.

Treats to help with training.

Water bowl. Stainless steel, non-tip are the best.

Food bowl.

Dog bed or rugs.

Toys. Activity toys that contain food are good for keeping a pup amused.

Collar and leash. The most secure collars are the soft webbing type, with a buckle for adjustment. (Clasp ones are designed for easy release, and when catching your dog by the collar, your hand could trigger the release buckle – this could be fatal if near a roadside.) Remember to keep checking the fit: pups grow quickly. Ideally, you should be able to insert a couple of fingers between collar and neck. Also do this with an older dog - he may gain or lose weight, so again, check the fit regularly. If you have a dog that likes getting wet, a leather collar may not be the best idea. Leather looks good, but unless looked after, will go hard and start to split. A webbing collar would be preferable: soft, yet hard wearing, ideal for a farm dog or one that likes swimming. I have used webbing collars for my own dogs – they are easy to wash. I do not recommend check chains, because unless used correctly, they can become choke chains (and as the chain tightens on the dog's neck he is almost strangled – I have even seen dogs vomiting when a check chain has been used). Accidents with check

A harness is ideal if space is limited – particularly useful in a two seater sports car.

chains do occur. The ring on the chain could get caught on a branch, fence or dense undergrowth and tighten around the dog's neck, causing death by strangulation if he were not discovered. Furthermore, if the chain becomes loose, then it could slip off your dog's neck and he could get lost without identification on him.

Dog tag. Even if you are getting your pup micro chipped, a tag clearly showing your address and phone number is essential. He could wander just a few streets away and be returned quickly as a result of such a precaution. A useful tip if you are going on holiday is to get a tag with either your holiday or your kennel's contact details.

Plenty of kitchen roll.

Poo bags. Nappy sacks are

good; keep some spare ones with you in the car.

Dog coat. A short haired dog may well need a coat in the winter months. Make sure it is waterproof – as a dog gets older he will appreciate not getting wet.

Car harness or, even better, a travelling crate. If your dog gets stressed in a vehicle, he may chew through a harness (and, on a long journey, could get agitated if the straps felt uncomfortable). With a crate, your dog has more freedom of movement – he can turn round, lie down or sit up, while safe and secure. Never let your dog roam loose around your vehicle.

Stair gate. Pups are clumsy. They should not be climbing stairs at a young age. Maybe they shouldn't be upstairs anyway?

THINK THROUGH YOUR CHOICE OF DOG

Taking on a rescue dog – typically from a rescue centre – is a wonderful way to acquire a pet. Be aware, however, that you will probably have to live with someone else's bad training. Of course, there are many problems associated with rescue dogs. They may not have been socialized or allowed to play, and might have been treated very badly. You will need to start from scratch, patiently following the guidelines in the previous and following chapters. You will be tempted to break training rules in order to compensate for the rough time your dog may have had. It is more important than ever not to let your heart rule your head. If, as your new dog settles, he doesn't see a clear pack leader (see page 35), then he may become aggressive. If he is naturally nervous, do not constantly reassure him that all is well. He is likely to misinterpret this, and think that there is a problem or sense that you lack confidence. Reassure him a

Regardless of breed, your dog will enjoy training with you.

little by all means, but be sure to treat situations that make him nervous in a no-nonsense manner. On the other hand, take things slowly, and try to avoid situations that you know will make him frightened.

Build his confidence step by step. Taking him to school may well be a good idea, but ask the trainer for a one-to-one session: a room full of other dogs could spook him badly. Expect it to take a long time to achieve the happy, confident dog you want. The rewards of success with a rescue dog are incomparable, and many a best friend has had a rough start to life.

CHECKLIST/THINGS TO DO BEFORE THE ARRIVAL OF YOUR PUP OR DOG

- Go round the garden and look for escape routes. Remember, a small, determined puppy can squeeze through the narrowest gaps.
- If you have a bar gate it is a good idea to mesh it – a puppy could get his head stuck.
- Move cleaning products out of reach – you could even put child locks on doors. Dogs get bored if they are left alone for too long, and a new dog will want to investigate all areas. I know of dogs that have even managed to open the fridge. It is not a good idea to leave your dog unattended in the kitchen, as a curious dog could open a cupboard and start chewing. My own dog Gal had that habit when I first got her from the rescue centre – and she soon discovered where I kept the cat food. Fortunately, she did not get into the cupboard containing cleaning products, which could have had disastrous results.
- Register with a vet, and arrange for your dog to have jabs. Ensure you put the vet's telephone number in a prominent place.
- Sort out pet insurance.

I have always had rescue dogs, often the worst cases. I had just lost my old dog, Luger, to old age and was distraught, when a friend who worked at the rescue kennels told me about an extremely traumatised German Shepherd Dog who faced being put down or living his life in the kennels. I couldn't get him out of my mind. He was so aggressive that no one could get near him – he had been in kennels for two weeks, having been dumped on the streets. During those two weeks he didn't wag his tail once, and the rescue centre had failed to notice he only had one testicle. When I went to see him, he flew at me, teeth bared. I put him on a leash and walked him. Afterwards he licked my hand, and our partnership began. I named him Soni. The poor dog was so frightened that he wouldn't go outside in the dark, and the first time I took him into dog school he tried to attack everyone (he did get verbally chastised on that occasion). Everyone had to ignore him for two months, then, gradually, the trainers were allowed to offer him a treat. Every day he grew in confidence, with me as the pack leader. Trust developed. Play was a very important part of his training, and it was through this that we established a bond, and started to watch each other's body language. The training was mainly done one-to-one to make concentration easier. The rest is history. Soni now

Taking in a rescue dog can be hard work, but is often the most rewarding.

helps round up the cattle, has done modelling work and appeared on a TV series. His tail now wags constantly. My other dog, Gal, also came from a rescue kennel. She had been locked in a shed and beaten. Gal was hyperactive, so finding the right home was essential. Again, I had just lost another dog, Luttie, to old age, when a friend told me about Gal. She, too, came home, and Soni was delighted to have a playmate. Once again, time, patience and training turned her into a great dog.

Not all rescue dogs are crossbreeds. Many pedigree dogs are thrown out.

Rescue dogs Soni and Gal working with cattle.

PUPPY'S ARRIVAL

Don't get all the relatives or neighbours round on the first day, as your pup needs time to familiarise himself with his surroundings. It's courteous to warn neighbours of your pup's arrival, and apologise in advance for any short-term disturbances. Perhaps keep a bottle of wine in stock, or strike up a deal with the local florist. Let them know that you are going to be a responsible owner.

Put on your puppy's collar – do it as quickly as you can and don't make a big deal of this or he may become upset. You may find that he tries to scratch or paw it off because it feels alien to him. Don't worry, he will soon forget all about it, so leave it on, then play with him to distract him. Or, put the collar on just as you are about to feed him. This way the food will act as a distraction.

Your pup may be tired after the journey: if he wants to sleep then let him. As soon as he wakes up, take him outside: he should be ready to relieve himself.

When you eat, ignore him,

Use a soft leash or even a piece of string (the lighter the better) to start with. If it is too heavy it will impede your pup's movements, and this will worry him. His first experience of a leash should not make him feel as though he is towing something as heavy as a truck.

and do not give any titbits from your plate. If he sits looking at the food, ignore him. If he is persistent, show displeasure with your facial expression; perhaps even give a growl. He can start learning about your body language right now.

Plan ahead. Occasionally put the leash on him and take him outside to get him used to it. Perhaps play with toys in order to distract him.

BEDTIME

Where would you like your adult dog to sleep? Your bed or bedroom is not a good idea. There is no need to spell out the reasons.

Choose the most suitable room, then decide what he is going to sleep on. There are many beds from which to choose, in all shapes and sizes, so think ahead to the size your dog may grow to. (I feel great pity for a dog whose feet, or should I say paws, stick out from the bottom of the bed.) Many people spend more time choosing their dog's bed than their own, and a bed is a personal choice. Rugs make good beds, especially if space is limited, and they are easy to vacuum, wash and transport. You can also coordinate a rug with the rest of the room and, of course, it can be walked on. A soft, simulated sheepskin rug will be easy to wash – a gorgeous, Persian rug (although it might look great) will show all the dog hairs. Ideally, having a rug in each room will give your dog plenty of comfortable places in which to settle. To keep a small puppy secure and snug, you could put a small rug in a puppy crate/cage or even in a box.

If you must have your dog in the bedroom, put the

A crate should be big enough for the pup or dog to stand up in and move around.

rug/cage/box at the bottom of the bed or at one side. Do not give in to the pup that tries to get on the bed: if he is persistent and determined then you must be too. If you give in once, next time it will be harder to resist. The first few nights are the hardest for you and the new pup, and it is easy to let your heart rule your head. Your pup has come from his Mum and possibly brothers and sisters, so he is naturally going to feel bewildered and upset.

Get a big cuddly toy and put that in the box. If pitiful night cries start, *ignore* them. If you go to reassure your pup, from then on he *will* call and call until you respond. Night cries will stop, your pup will settle eventually, though every pup is different and some will settle more easily than others. Try putting an old towel under your jumper for a couple of hours before bedtime to pick up your scent. Leave this in the pup's box or cage. A ticking clock, or a radio left on quietly might also give some reassurance. If he howls like a banshee for hours, cotton wool or earplugs might be the only answer.

After a good night's sleep, a puppy will be lively and very keen to greet the new family. Too much excitement at an early stage will lead to a rather boisterous, overbearing older dog that mugs everyone on sight. So, use a gentle voice for your morning greeting, and then take him straight outside for a pee. It is extra important, at this moment, to get your body language right. Show real pleasure on your face when the deed is done.

Puppies need plenty of sleep, so if he sleeps late, enjoy the peace and leave him well alone. If he has peed overnight, don't shout or get annoyed: just clean up. A puppy cannot control his bowels for hours: you would not expect this of a baby, and nor should you of a puppy.

Your pup will feel safe and secure in his own bed or blanket.

CHAPTER THREE

SETTING THE RULES

BREAKFAST TIME

Get your pup to sit and wait for his food by using the word "Stay", and the stay signal (palm held upwards facing pup - see page 17). Put his food down, say "OK" and carry on doing your own thing. It is important not to make a big deal out of feed times.

Many owners make the mistake of touching the dog and then removing his food before he has finished. They do this to prove that they can take food off their dog. This can make the animal anticipate the removal of food, and could make him aggressive. Instead, put a little food in the bowl and tell him to wait. When he is calm, praise him and put the bowl down. When he has eaten it all, pick up the bowl and repeat. Again, don't make a big deal of this. It doesn't need to be done every meal time, only occasionally. At other times, give the complete feed and leave him well alone, getting on with your jobs and leaving him to eat in peace. Ignore him and only walk past occasionally. Give him a pat on the head and a "Good boy": no more. Dogs hate interference while eating. If your dog does not eat with enthusiasm, or

WHO EATS FIRST?

In an ideal world, you, the pack leader, eat first. But, with a young dog on three to four feeds a day this is unrealistic. There is an easy solution: mix the pup's food, then eat something small (perhaps a piece of fruit), then let him eat.

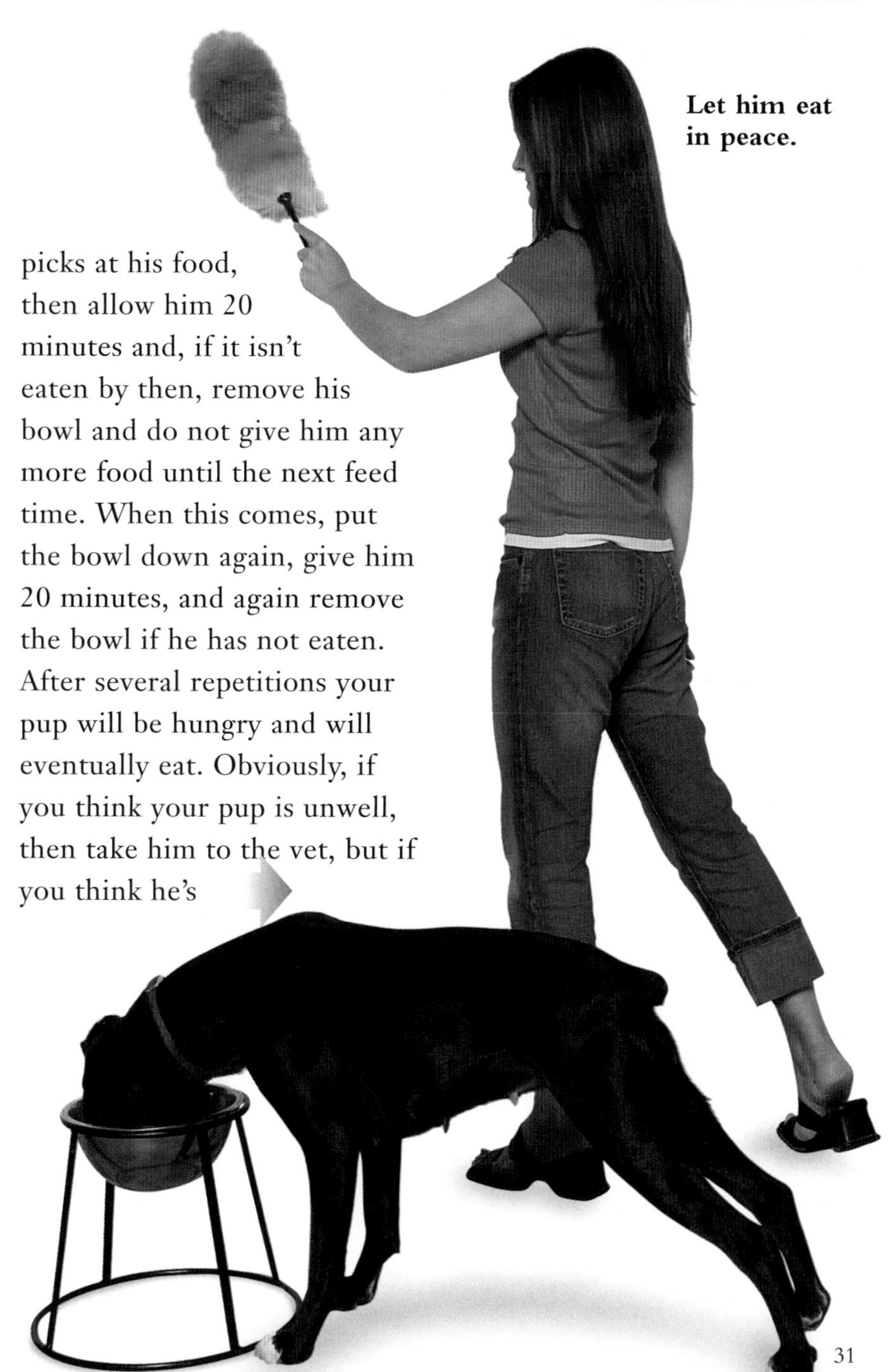

Let him eat in peace.

picks at his food, then allow him 20 minutes and, if it isn't eaten by then, remove his bowl and do not give him any more food until the next feed time. When this comes, put the bowl down again, give him 20 minutes, and again remove the bowl if he has not eaten. After several repetitions your pup will be hungry and will eventually eat. Obviously, if you think your pup is unwell, then take him to the vet, but if you think he's

This pup is ready to eat. Rather than letting him get over excited, it is better to teach him some manners and patience.

bored with the food you usually give, don't make the mistake of changing it. Whatever you do, don't start buying lots of different feeds: you will end up with a fussy eater who will only eat the best steak. In all my years with dogs I have never known a dog commit suicide through starvation when there is a bowl of dog food available.

If, when you are eating, your pup looks on and drools, ignore him. If he is persistent to the point of pawing or barking, you could let out a small growl, then ignore him once again. If you don't give in, then the pup learns that this behaviour gets him nowhere. You may think it's cute, but if you give in he will see your behaviour as weak. I have a rule in my house: I don't eat my dogs` dinner, and they don't eat mine.

Although this dog looks hungry, he also looks well fed. No sharing.

WARNING

Some visitors (possibly your parents) find a cute, new pup so irresistible (and think you so mean for not giving in), that they slip him a morsel when you are not looking. When he has grown up and drools on their best clothes, they will not be so understanding. If this happens, enjoy telling them that the dog doesn't do it with you. Encourage them to join you in a short training session – they'll like being involved.

DANGER

Chocolate is poisonous to dogs. It contains theobromine which the human system can metabolize efficiently, but the canine system can't. As dogs struggle to excrete the substance, it affects their central nervous system, cardiovascular system and blood pressure – placing severe strain on their bodies, even to the point of causing death.

TIME TO GO OUT

In an ideal world you would stay in all the time and never leave your dog alone. But, of course, this is impossible. When you have to leave the house, don't make a big fuss of pup. You probably feel like saying: "Now you be a good boy, I won't be long." Try not to do this: it will make your pup feel confused when you do actually leave. Instead, ignore him for about 15 minutes before leaving, then just go. This sends the message: 'my going out is nothing special.' In the end, such an approach will give you a much more resilient, easygoing animal.

Remove anything chewable, such as the TV remote control, from the room that your pup will occupy. To deter him from chewing you could smear vinegar or alcohol on wooden furniture. Once again, a puppy crate can be a good solution: no chewed furniture, and because dogs don't like to

'Come on, I'm in charge.'

soil their beds, a crate can help with toilet training. Think before leaving him alone with a toy. Could it be ripped up and swallowed? Think ahead: a chewed piece could get stuck in his throat and make him choke. There are some useful toys on the market into which you insert food. The dog has to roll the toy around the floor until it dispenses a treat.

An hour or so before going out, try to put aside a few minutes' play time for your pup: throw some toys in order to use up some of his energy – this could make him sleepy later. Then go through the routine of ignoring him and leaving without making a fuss, as described on page 33. From now on, accept that you will have to get up at least half an hour earlier than in the past to make sure that you have this extra time. It's unfair to expect your pup to sleep when he is still full of energy.

If you are out for more

than a couple of hours, get someone to come in and stay with your dog for a while: they should let him into the garden and play with him, but they, like you, must settle him back in his cage and ignore him for a while before leaving, or he may start howling and barking in order to call them back.

This is harmful to the dog, and unpleasant for both of you.

PACK LEADERS

Pack leaders should have two legs not four. A four-legged pack leader:

- Begs and gets food from other pack members.
- Gets attention on demand. If your dog comes to you for a fuss, ignore him, even if he keeps nudging your hand. Call him to you a little later, and fuss over him. Stop when you have had enough. This puts you firmly in charge.
- Sleeps where he wants.
- Instigates play.
- Goes through a door first.
- Follows you everywhere, even to the bathroom. (Just shut the door, and when you come out, ignore him.)
- Pulls on the leash.
- Comes back only when it suits him.

Do you really want your dog to be the pack leader?

IF A PUPPY BITES...

If your pup bites your fingers, it does not mean he is bound to be aggressive. He is simply attention seeking. The worst response you can have is to smack the pup's nose: this is aggressive body language, and aggression encourages aggression. If a child comes to stroke your dog, all your dog will see is a hand approaching his nose. So, in order to prevent a smack, he may bite.

Young children can badly confuse a puppy who nips, by waving their arms and screaming. This body language can be misconstrued as fun. You, the adult, should take control by removing the puppy until things calm down.

If your pup bites your hand, yelp and turn away. This negative body language is what the animal must see. Reinforce it by ignoring him. If he persists, remove him, gently but firmly, from the situation. If he still persists, every time he starts biting your hand, as he takes hold of it, grab his top or bottom jaw and squeeze gently. When he starts to whimper, release your grip but keep your hand there. He should then move back from your hand. If you offer it to him again, he should not respond. If he does, then repeat this. From your pup's point of

The face has a look of displeasure and the body language is not welcoming. A really negative signal.

view, it now hurts when he bites. Never snatch your hand away from him, or it will become a game and the biting will get worse.

There is no need to resort to this technique unless you have a major problem with biting. Your facial expression should show displeasure, followed by a happy face when he stops.

HOUSE TRAINING

Your pup has little natural control of his bladder or bowels for the first months of his life, and it is standard practice to leave him a litter tray lined with paper (if possible, leave this by the back door). Empty it in the garden in a place where you would like him to perform in future. When he picks up the scent, he will get the idea that this is a good place for relieving himself. During this toilet training period, you will need eyes in the back of your head. The signs to look for are: sniffing the floor, looking at the door, going round in circles. At the first sign, take your puppy outside, give the command "Empty", and praise if he responds. Of course, some pups just go without warning. Don't worry, it really does stop as the pup grows up. Never shout – this may start a vicious circle: your pup will become nervous and even less able than usual to control his bladder. Just be vigilant, and take him outside every couple of hours.

OLDER DOGS

It is not unusual for an older dog to relieve himself in a new home for the first few days. This does not mean that he isn't house trained, it is most likely to be nerves, and the need for a familiar scent to create a feeling of security. Use the same technique discussed above, and be extra patient. My own rescue dog soiled my bed, even though he was fully housetrained.

HOME COMING

The greeting you receive when you return home is one of the great joys of owning a dog, but you do not want your clothes ripped, legs scratched or your shopping spread all over the floor. So, guard against this scenario by ignoring your pup for about five minutes when you first walk in. Make a cup of tea, glance at the paper, or put the shopping away. When he is calm, make a fuss of him and spend some quality time with him. Once your pup realizes that jumping up and biting at clothes gets no attention, and calmness does, he will just wag his tail when you arrive and not get over-excited. As with all aspects of training, prevention is better than cure.

VISITORS

Like it or not, visitors will arrive, sometimes unannounced. Everyone loves a cute pup, but visitors often need controlling as much as the dog. They, like you, must ignore him for a while after they first come through the door.

So, while your pup is young, introduce him to

strangers, but don't make a big deal out of it. If possible, know in advance what time they'll arrive, and have your pup on a leash. Jumping up must be ignored: but let them pat him and talk to him for a brief second before ignoring him. Visitors must not be regarded as a threat. Window cleaners, odd-job men and builders are perhaps the biggest problem because they come right into a dog's territory. If you can take your pup outside on a leash to see them, he can begin to adjust to their presence. As usual, don't make a big deal of the event. Once the workman is indoors, encourage the pup to come and play with you for a short time whilst he gets used to this new person being in the house. Distraction, as ever,

As your pup gets familiar with visitors, you could even teach him to collect the mail. This could be useful in wet weather – as long as the mail does not end up in a puddle when your pup is distracted by the lovely dog from next door.

is the key, so that he can get used to strangers' noise and movements in his own time. You want to avoid him getting over-excited and barking in anticipation of guests. Remember that people in uniform have been known to spook or even frighten puppies. If your pup looks worried, you must act confidently and tell the person in uniform just to ignore your pup and avoid towering over him. Act calmly, and your puppy will too.

FIRST WALK OUT

Having already got your pup used to a leash, going on a first walk is a major step. Take him somewhere quiet for the first few walks, away from heavy traffic. Stop at the kerbs and make him sit or stand, so he gets used to stopping. (A sit is not always

Have your poo bags ready, and take toys for every walk.

practical if the weather is wet.) The commotion of a big lorry can spook your pup, so get him used to traffic from a distance. Take a favourite toy and some treats with you, and of course, a bag for droppings.

An older, male dog will constantly try to cock his leg in order to mark territory. It really is antisocial to let your dog do this on other people's property, so keep the pace up and don't stop. If he tries to cock his leg, give the "No" command, in a firm voice.

Don't try and imitate leg-cocking in order to make him do this where you would like him to. Dogs just think you're being weird, or funny.

When you reach the spot where it is fine for him to go, give the "Empty" command (or whatever word you choose), and praise when he responds.

Find somewhere safe, away from the road, where your pup

Use two toys to keep your dog's attention.

can have a free run. Play throwing the toy, using the opportunity to interact with him. Take two toys. If he won't come back with the first one, show him the second, tease him with it, but don't throw it until he has come back to you and released the first toy (either by giving it to you or at least dropping it on the ground). If you bend down and look as if you are examining the ground, your pup will be curious to see what you are doing and will come over. When he comes, give him a treat and plenty of praise. If your pup appears to be wandering away, run in the

Pretending to examine something on the ground should attract your pup's attention - he will want to see what you are doing.

opposite direction, calling him to you. Again, when he comes give plenty of praise.

Encouraging your dog to go with you, rather than you chasing him.

Bending down to a pup's level, arms outstretched, is inviting. Plenty of praise.

DANGER

Never encourage your dog to play with sticks: there's a real risk from splinters; or, worse, if a dog runs with a stick and suddenly stops, the stick can stab him in the throat or chest. I know of two dogs that were killed when playing with sticks.

Solid rubber balls are also dangerous: they get covered in saliva and when a dog runs with them, tossing his head in the air, the ball can slither down his throat and block his airway. It is difficult to retrieve the ball from his throat before he suffocates.

Stones are not good for dogs: they chip the teeth and can get swallowed (resulting in a traumatic trip to the vet for an operation).

Your dog will be less inclined to wander off if he is having fun with you.

LIVING HARMONIOUSLY

CATS AND DOGS

Cats and dogs can live in harmony – it is usually the cat that is in charge, but remember: ultimately, you must be in control. If you already have a cat and are bringing a dog into the house for the first time, take him in on a leash. Your cat will probably spit and hiss at him. Keep calm. If your dog reacts by growling or barking, give a gentle tug on the collar and tell him "No". Turn him to you so he can see your body language, and when he responds, praise him. For the first few days, keep him on his leash whenever the cat is about. He will soon learn the cat's body language: for example, that a cat waves its tail in anger, not play. Gradually they should get used to each other.

If there's already a dog in the house, and the cat is the new arrival, keep the cat in its travelling box or a cage when the dog is about.

Again, keep the dog on the leash for extra control. A new cat has to be kept inside for at least a couple of weeks anyway, in order for it to get to know its territory. When you sense that your dog is losing interest in the cat, take the leash off and let him go to the cat cage. If your dog is not bothered by the cat's presence, then after a while you can try letting the cat out – but first put the leash back on the dog. Once again: prevention is better than cure. Many dogs will accept a cat quickly; with others you will need to be patient and make sure that the cat has an escape route – typically a higher place to which it can jump.

Dogs and cats often end up sleeping in the same bed and even playing together.

Even in a home environment dogs feel their pack instinct. They can learn to regard every household member – cats included – as part of their own pack. Once they do, they won't feel the need to chase the cat.

DOGS AND THE FAMILY

Growing up with a dog is wonderful for a child. Children need to realise, though, that the dog is not a toy. I cannot count how many times I have heard how 'wonderful' the dog is with the kids: "They can

The bond formed here will last a lifetime. Memories are made of such relationships.

pull his ears, jump on him and he is ever so good". Sometimes I can't believe what I hear. Children should be taught from an early age how to treat a dog. Involve them in the feeding and training, but always supervise them. If the dog is resting or asleep, they should leave him alone. After all, children don't like to be disturbed when they are resting. A crawling baby's body language may look like a play signal to a dog. Never leave the two alone together.

A dog that is usually wonderful with children can have his off days: he may simply be under the weather, or feel stressed by all the attention. It is important to provide your dog with a place to rest where the children are not allowed to go. It is not a good idea to leave a young child alone with a dog, no matter how good they both are. Young children can be unintentionally cruel – after all, they injure themselves by inserting objects in all sorts of places. Furthermore, children tease each other, and it's all part of growing up, but to tease a dog may well lead to a nip or bite. Dogs can be remarkably tolerant, but their patience does have limits, and unfortunately for the dog, one bite can mean rejection from the family. Because small children can be the same height as a dog, bites to the face are not unusual.

Both dog and child are having fun. Encouraging the child to play correctly with the dog is essential. No teasing.

INTRODUCING A NEW BABY

I get angry when I hear people say "We're having a baby, so we need to get rid of the dog." Why? Your dog is a member of the family, so why should he have to go? Before getting a dog, people should consider whether they will be happy to accommodate an animal as well as a young family. You must plan ahead, and avoid the 'dog-baby' being replaced by the human baby.

When you start bringing home baby equipment, let your dog see it. Give the command "Leave" gently, combined with praising body language. He will soon learn not to bother with it. Carry a doll around from time to time and make baby noises to it. This sounds silly, but it will familiarise your dog with what is to come. If he

The dog is naturally inquisitive with a new family member. Everyone is relaxed – the dog is picking up this body language from the other family members.

reacts by jumping up and getting excited, you must not react. Ignore him, using negative body language.

Go for a walk with the pushchair to get him used to trotting alongside it. Take him for a walk past playing fields or schools, so he can get used to the noise children make. When you bring the baby home, he is going to be curious, especially when the baby cries. Act

Training with a pushchair prior to your baby's arrival is a good idea. Perhaps you could borrow a friend's child, or use an empty pushchair.

calmly and let him sniff the baby's blanket in order to get used to the new scent. At first, keep your dog on a leash so he can familiarise himself with the baby while under control. Dogs can become highly protective of a baby, and will often alert you if the baby cries. In fact, they can worry over a crying baby. But they usually adjust soon enough. Don't stop giving your dog the usual amount of attention and exercise, and all should be well. Dogs are quick to learn that a toddler's feeding time can be rewarding: food is thrown about, and he benefits.

ONE DOG OR TWO?

Dogs enjoy each other's company and having two dogs can be wonderful – but potentially double the trouble. It is important to get your first dog trained before taking on a second one – they learn from each other and you want the second to pick up good habits from the first. If your first dog is aggressive or runs off, for example, then your new dog

Two young dogs from the same home should be trained separately to walk without pulling. Each dog needs individual attention to get the best out of him.

When training, have a break to let your dog interact with his friends. Keep him on a leash during the break so that when you start to train again it is easy to get him to focus on you. This will also teach your dog that you are the leader and make the decisions about when to play and when to work.

will end up doing the same.

It is not a good idea to take a new dog straight into your established dog's home for the first meeting, as it is more than likely that your dog will resent the new dog for invading his patch, and he could well show aggression. If possible, introduce the two to each other on neutral territory, such as a local park or field, to discover how they are likely to get along. If this first meeting goes well and they seem friendly towards each other, the new dog will be accepted more easily when entering the family home.

If you need to command one dog but not the other, focus your body language on him and ignore the other. Try to get eye contact with him, and use his name.

TRAINING

This section is the biggest and most important in the book, offering a complete step-by-step training course, modelled on how we train in my own school.

TRAINING SESSION BASICS

Ensure you have treats and a toy. These should always be close to hand: big pockets or a bum bag are the answer.

Trousers are best for training, as you will bend down often. Wear a short jacket that will not flap in your dog's face. Choose comfortable clothes that give freedom of movement.

A little bit too distracting for a training school.

Not ideal for bending down, and the shoes could injure a dog.
Keep the coat fastened as you need to see your dog and vice-versa.

The ideal dress for training: both fashionable and comfortable. Easier now to concentrate on the dog.

Now is when body language comes into its own. Your voice should be calm, firm and low for commands, higher for praise. You need to be constantly aware of, and making use of, voice and body language. The exercises on the following pages are (or should be) taught at training schools, but they are also for practising at home. Remember: at training school a dog has more than the usual number of distractions, so don't be in a hurry to remove his leash.

In schools, dogs are taught on the left hand side of the handler. This goes back to the days of 'dog on the left, gun on the right.' If you are left handed you may find this awkward, but once you are familiar with the body language it will get easier. In my school there is a young girl who, due to a disability, does all her training with her dog on the right. Her training is done in mirror fashion to everyone else's, but her dog understands her body language because she is consistent with it throughout.

Dogs have a natural need to release energy, and thrive on plenty of physical exercise. Your relationship will benefit if you give him this.

EXERCISE 1: THE SIT

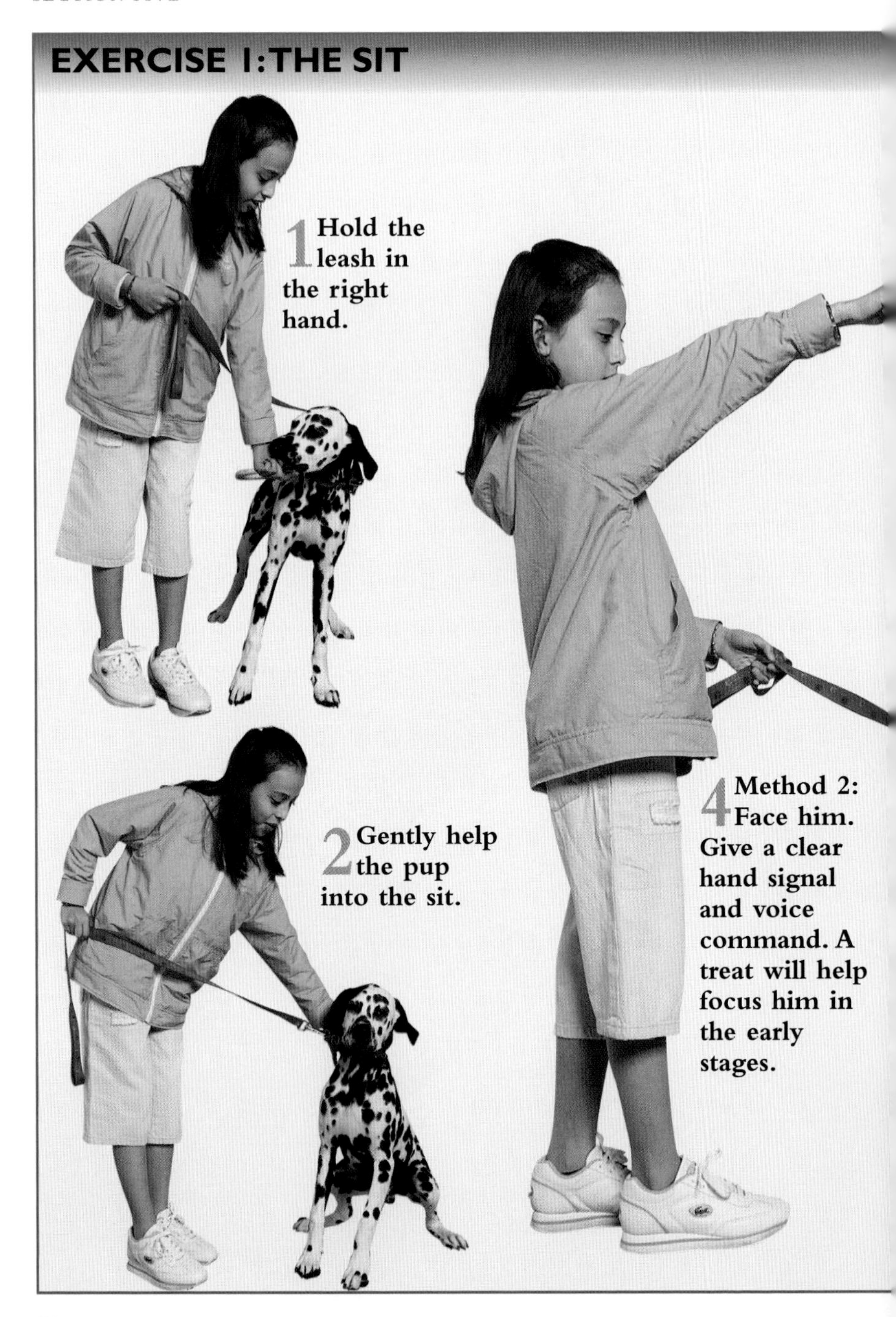

1 Hold the leash in the right hand.

2 Gently help the pup into the sit.

4 Method 2: Face him. Give a clear hand signal and voice command. A treat will help focus him in the early stages.

3 Praise and reward him.

THE SIT

Perhaps you have mastered the sit already, but there is no harm in consolidating this basic command.

Hold the leash in your right hand with the dog on your left, and give the command "Sit". Gently raise the leash and with your left hand ease him into the sit. Praise as soon as he responds. Bend at the knees rather than from the waist: leaning over him could be taken as threatening body language.

IMPORTANT

Look at the trainer's body language and facial expressions in every photo, noting how the dog responds.

EXERCISE 2: THE DOWN PART 1

1 Method one: start from the sit.

2 Place the left outstretched hand on his back, but do not push. Use a calm but firm voice "Down".

3 **Make sure the treat stays by your dog's nose.**

4 **Move the treat forward slowly.**

EXERCISE 2: THE DOWN PART 2

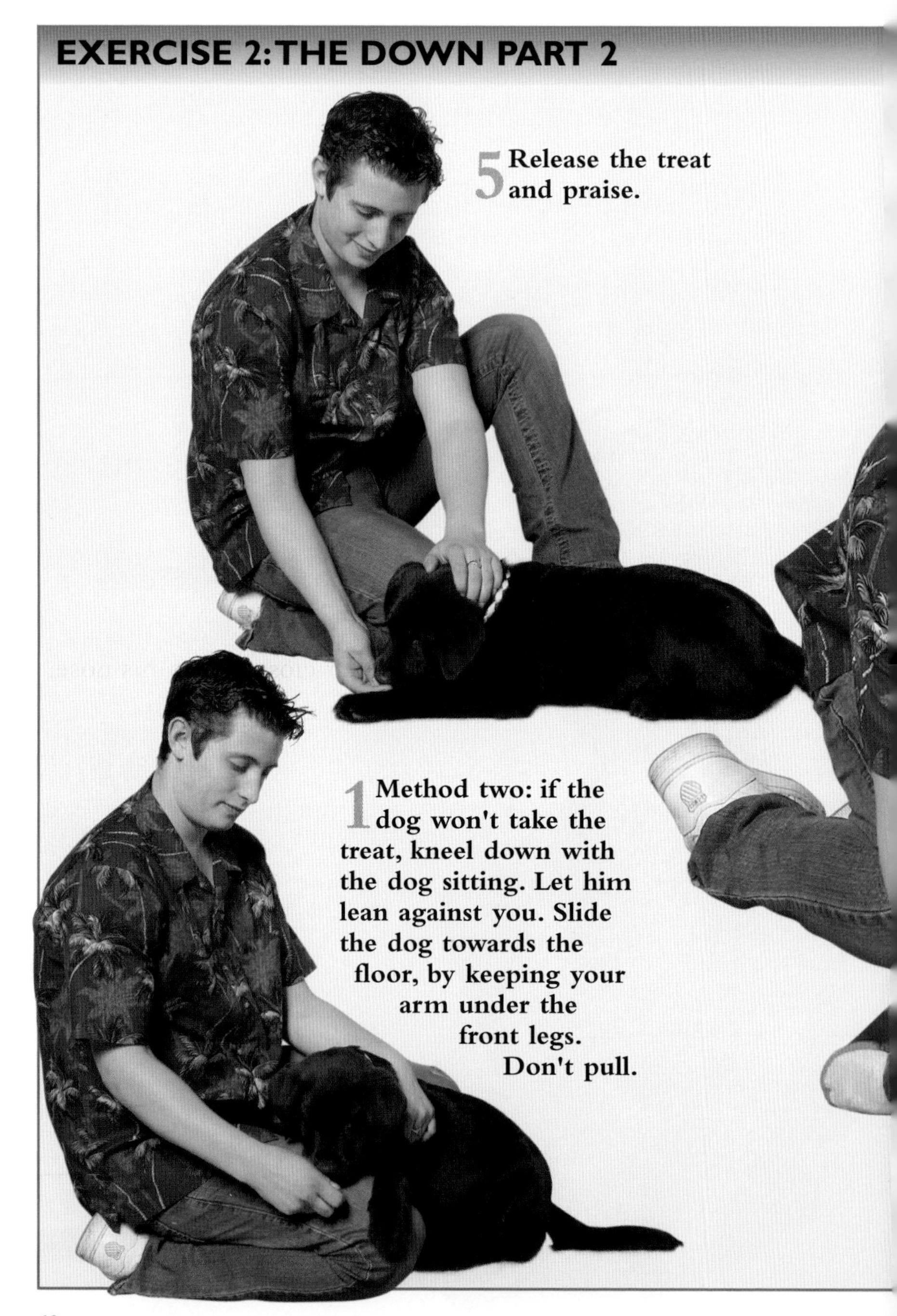

5 Release the treat and praise.

1 Method two: if the dog won't take the treat, kneel down with the dog sitting. Let him lean against you. Slide the dog towards the floor, by keeping your arm under the front legs. Don't pull.

2 **Stroke the dog and praise.**

THE DOWN

The down is important, because putting the dog in a submissive position will help him learn who is the pack leader (see page 35). First, get the pup to sit on your left. Then get down beside him (by doing this your body language is not threatening), gently placing your left outstretched hand on his shoulders. With the right hand, place a treat under his nose, then lower it to the floor. The pup will follow it closely with his nose. Don't move the treat away from his nose or he will stand up. Give the vocal command "Down". Lower it gently towards his front legs, and then gradually move it forwards. This will make him lie right down. Now release the treat and praise. Once your pup has mastered this you can stay standing: he will be happy to respond to your confident upright body language and hand signal commands.

THE STAYS

Having a dog that will do good stays is extremely beneficial, and you will discover that the command has many uses. You may, for example, need to speak to someone who is a little scared of dogs. If your dog is sitting still, this will reassure them that he is not a threat.

With the sit stay, your dog will be watching your body language very closely in case you will call him to you, or return to him.

The down stay is different. After giving the command you always return to your dog. He will be relaxed and will wait for you if he understands that you will always return to his side when he is in the down position. The down stay is particularly useful if you have to attend to a problem or a dangerous situation when you are out with your dog: putting him in the down stay ensures that he'll stay there while you sort things out.

When I was out walking recently, I needed to help an elderly walker who had fallen down. His own dog was distressed, so it was best to keep mine out of the way. Fortunately, the walker was just a little shaken and, after a few minutes, was able to continue on his way. My dog stayed in the down for what must have seemed a very long time to him, but it made the situation easier to handle.

THE SIT STAY

Position him on your left. Give the sit command. Hold the leash in your left hand. Using your right hand, show its upright palm to the dog. Give the command "Stay". Moving the right leg, take a step to face your dog. If your dog tries to move towards you, apply some tension to the leash to prevent him from moving. After just a few seconds, step back to the original position at your dog's right side. Count to three.

SPORTING DOGS

These dogs make wonderful companions, and are a pleasure to train because they pick up body language easily. They enjoy going out in all weather and like to be involved in as much activity as possible. When you start training a sporting dog, do plenty of controlled leash work, if possible by a pond or lake. They love to swim (the dirtier the water the better), so it is crucial to gain control near water early on. Well-known breeds in this group include the Golden Retreiver (pictured) and the Springer Spaniel. This dog (and any dog when out of doors) should be wearing a collar and tag.

EXERCISE 3: SIT STAYS

1 Keep the body upright. Firmly command: "Stay".

2 Step away with the right foot. Keep the hand steady, looking at your dog as you walk away.

4 Return, keeping the body upright and the hand signal steady.

Give the vocal command "OK" (this is the release command) and praise.

If he moves on your return, then put him back in the sit. Count to three before releasing him. Then say "OK" and praise. Don't try to walk too far away, or for too long. Remember 'Stay' means 'Stay'.

If you try to progress too fast, you will never get him to do this properly. When you are confident that your dog understands, go further away and for longer.

Maintain the facial expression and the hand signal in combination with an upright, confident body. You should radiate confidence. Don't use your dog's name to get his attention, or move your hand, as he may think you are calling him and move towards you.

If, during the exercise, your dog moves, then go back to the last stage and repeat it until your dog is ready to progress. Never laugh if he

PASTORAL / HERDING DOGS

All breeds in this group share the ability to control the movement of other animals, often showing this instinct when out on a walk because they keep the group together. They respond beautifully to training. Well-known herding breeds include the Border Collie (pictured below) and the German Shepherd Dog. Less common are the Puli and Briard.

breaks his stay, or he will interpret your laughter as praise and get confused.

Practise sit stays little and often, but not so much as to bore your dog. If, during the exercise, your dog goes into the down position, return to him and gently but firmly put him back in the sit. Then carry on with the stay. Don't let your attention wander, or so will your dog's.

REMEMBER THE BODY SIGNALS

By using the right leg first when walking away from your dog in the stay position, and your left leg first for heel work, you teach your dog to read your body language. In time you should be able to move one leg and your dog will know whether to stay, or to walk to heel without the need for any vocal commands.

THE DOWN STAY

Use the same start method as with the sit stay. Put your dog into the down on your left side. Again, walk away with the right leg and turn to face your dog. Your body language will be different with the down. The hand command is a palm facing almost down. This is the one exercise in which your body can lean slightly forward from the waist, but you should not tower over your dog. As with the sit stay, return to your dog. Stand at his side. Count to three, say "OK", and praise.

Don't be in a rush to do this exercise off the leash: until you have control on it, you won't have control off. Once you have got to the stage where you can go as far as the end of the leash and your dog is staying happily, try moving about from side to side and circling your dog. Repeat the stay command at intervals, especially if you think he is going to move.

Once this exercise is completed, play with your dog. Training should be fun.

EXERCISE 4: DOWN STAYS

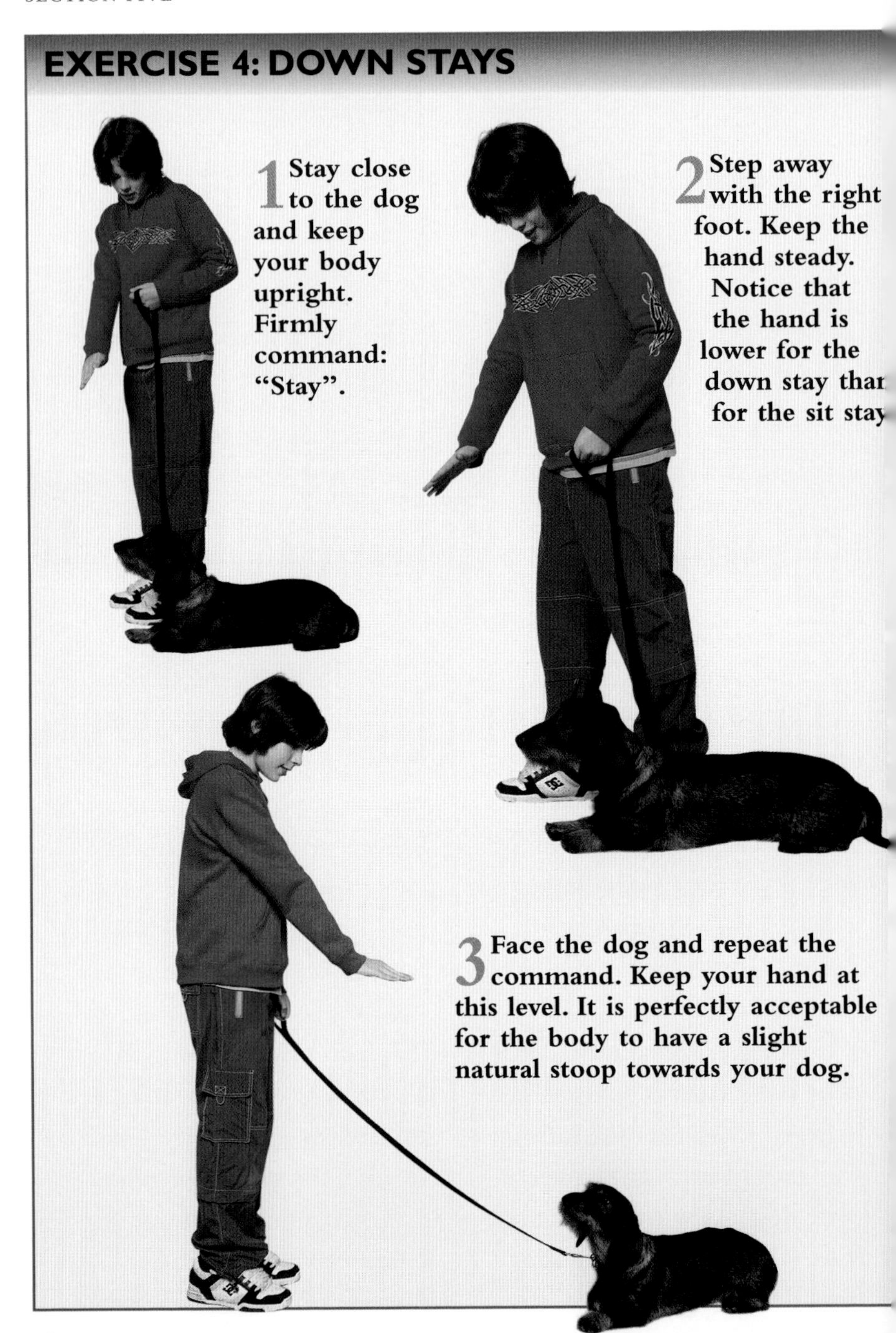

1 Stay close to the dog and keep your body upright. Firmly command: "Stay".

2 Step away with the right foot. Keep the hand steady. Notice that the hand is lower for the down stay than for the sit stay.

3 Face the dog and repeat the command. Keep your hand at this level. It is perfectly acceptable for the body to have a slight natural stoop towards your dog.

4 Return, keeping the hand signal steady.

5 Give a release command – "OK" – and praise the dog.

HEEL WORK

There is nothing worse than having your arm tugged constantly, and heel work makes your dog walk close to your heels. The ideal position for heel work is with your dog's shoulder level with your left leg. This takes up less room on the pavement and, if your dog stays in position, you won't trip over him.

Motivate your dog in the early stages of heel work with a treat. Put your dog on your left side, hold the leash slack in your left hand, and hold a treat in the right.

Your right hand should be level with your left leg (see page 72 for the puppy recall part 1). Give the command "Heel", and set off, left leg first. Keep the treat close to the dog's nose. Praise your dog for walking in the correct position. After several steps, give the command "Come". Move your hand to the centre of your legs and walk backwards a few steps. Stop, give the command "Sit" and release the treat. Praise him, get out a toy and play.

Every time your dog makes eye contact with you, give the excitable praise command. With this exercise you will wish you had a Great Dane, because keeping the treat close to your dog's nose is hard on the back with a small dog.

This whole exercise is called the puppy recall. It helps to teach your dog the correct heel position and, because it keeps him alert to your sudden change in body language as you go backwards, it is excellent for holding his attention. When training, slot in a few puppy recalls to break up the heelwork – this will make it less tedious for you both.

The next stage is harder (see page 78). Again, with your dog on your left, this time hold the leash in your right hand. Your right arm needs to be straight. Give the

Page 77

HOUNDS

This shows the lovely range of colours of Greyhounds. Hounds are brilliant at picking up scent – they were originally hunting dogs and like to work in a pack. The key to training Hounds is food, so always take a supply of smelly treats when training. Well-known Hound breeds include the Greyhound (pictured above) and the Whippet; less common are the Otterhound and the Borzoi.

EXERCISE 5: THE PUPPY RECALL PART 1

1 Keep the leash slack.

2 Treat is in your right hand, placed on the left leg at the height of your dog's nose.

3 Use plenty of encouragement and the command "Heel".

4 Move your hand to the centre of your legs.

EXERCISE 5: THE PUPPY RECALL PART 2

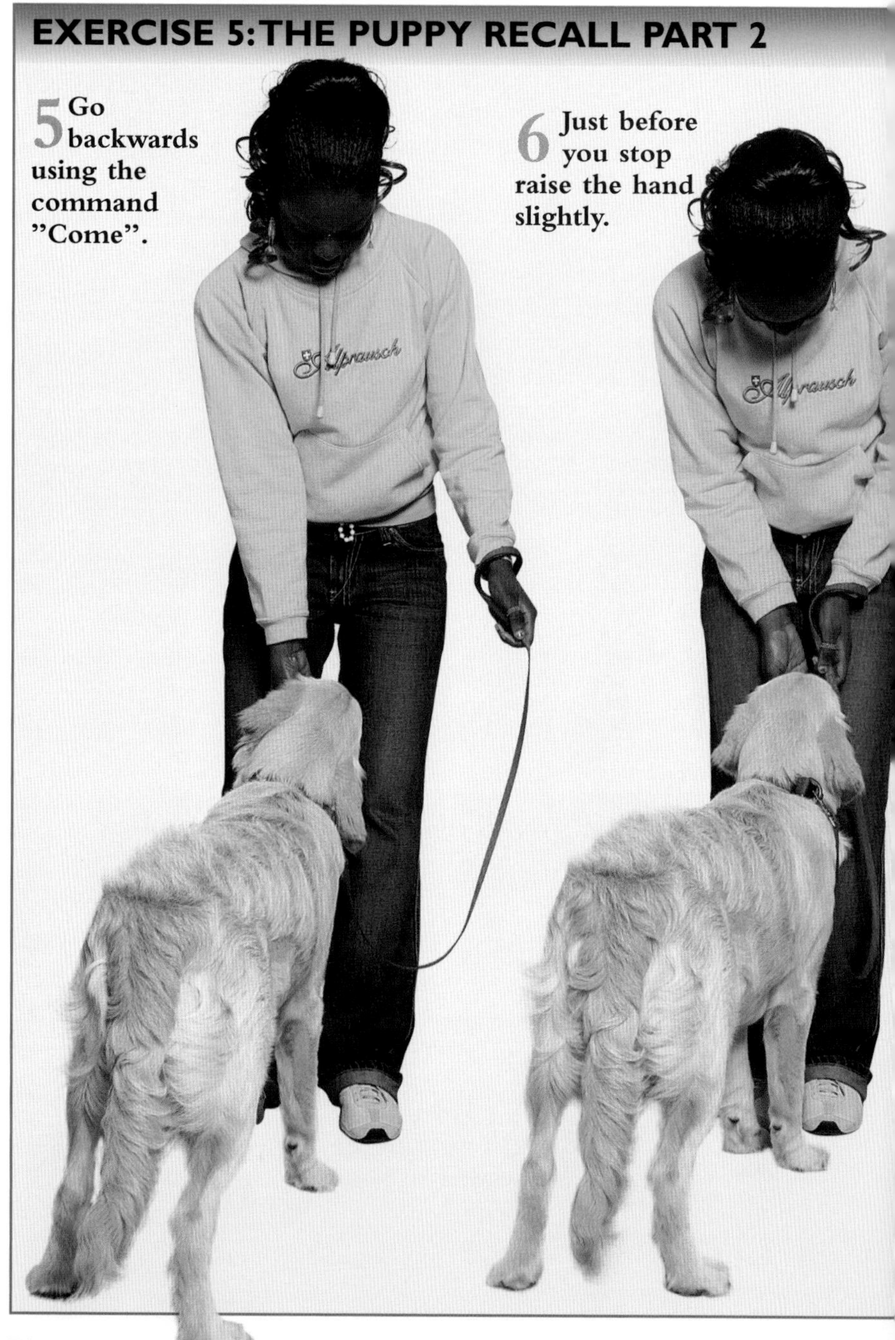

5 Go backwards using the command "Come".

6 Just before you stop raise the hand slightly.

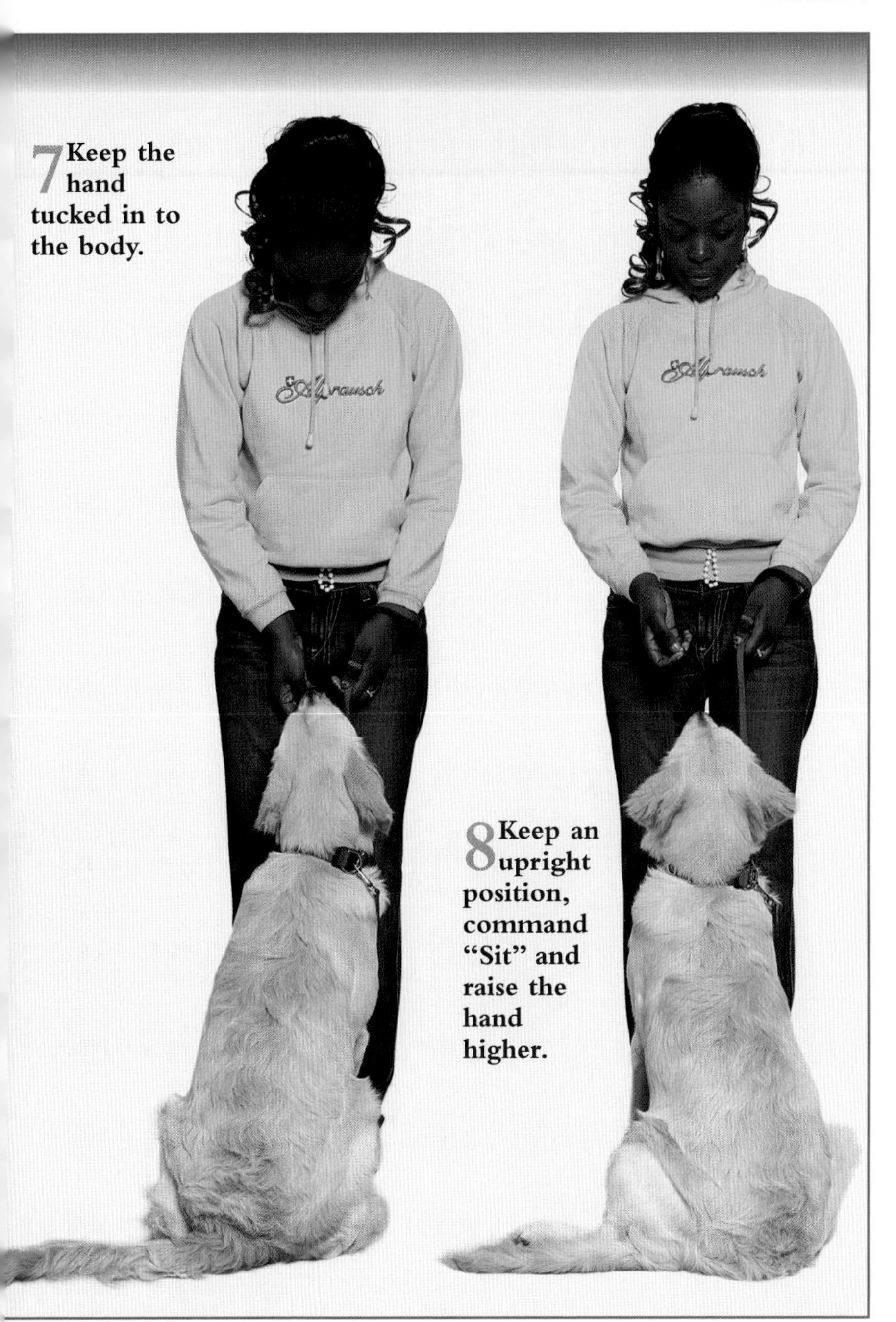

7 Keep the hand tucked in to the body.

8 Keep an upright position, command "Sit" and raise the hand higher.

Plenty of praise and a smile.

command in a firm tone: "Heel". Set off, left leg first. If your dog pulls ahead, say "Heel", then extend your arm forwards to put some slack in the leash. Give a gentle, quick pull to get him back into position. Praise in a higher tone.

Whenever your dog is in the correct position, look at him and give praise. The leash should always bc slack. Your arm should not come across your chest, but be level with your dog, almost resting on your left leg, so when you give a tug, your arm goes to your right leg and back again, and the dog receives a small tug to remind him not to pull.

In a training school you may find yourself walking with a dog in front and a dog behind, so you mustn't let his attention wander to the backside of the dog in front. Again, if he looks at you, offer excitable praise, or use a treat if this helps. It is important that you pay all your attention to your own dog. If you don't give 100 per cent then he won't either. If you're doing this exercise in a training school, resist the temptation to chat to another dog owner. You'll often (unconsciously) use hand gestures as you chat, and this can confuse a dog.

When walking behind other dogs during a training session, the dog in front may be distracted if you walk with your dog too close to him. He will keep turning round and may even get agitated if you invade his space. This is also unnerving for your own dog. Allow a gap of at least a few feet. The pace of heelwork may vary considerably if one dog and owner are moving slower than the rest of the group. So, if the dog in front slows down, you should too. Remember, you are all at training school for the same reason – life will be much easier if you are considerate of other dogs and their owners.

EXERCISE 6: WALKING TO HEEL PART 1

2 Holding the leash with the right hand across the body.

1 Remember to start off with the left leg.

3 The dog starts to pull, so give the vocal command "Heel".

EXERCISE 6: WALKING TO HEEL PART 2

4 Notice the slack in the leash.

5 The arm comes back, giving a gentle tug.

6 Dog in the heel position, and your arm has returned to its normal position.

UTILITY/ NON SPORTING DOGS

This is a diverse group, with great variations in size, appearance, personality and ability. They all tend to make good watchdogs and companions, but can be difficult to train, often appearing disinterested in learning. Persevere: find your dog's particular motivation (a certain treat or toy?) and you should get results. Well-known breeds in this group include the Dalmation (pictured) and the Bulldog. Less common are the Bichon Frise and the Tibetan Spaniel. This Dalmation is wearing a harness – not ideal if he is left to play outside, as it could catch, for example, on a branch.

EXERCISE 7: RIGHT TURN

1 Give the command "Heel" just before you make the turn.

2 Pat the left leg, and encourage.

3 **Praise on completion.**

THE RIGHT TURN

To make a right turn, use the word "Heel", turn to the right, dip your body slightly, pat your left leg to encourage your dog and make your turn. Praise and smile while continuing to walk. If you keep your body language simple, your dog will soon recognise the slight change in your posture. Don't exaggerate the dip of your body – keep your body language as natural as you would normally when making a turn. Develop this exercise by letting him off the leash, allowing him to play close by. Turn and face another direction, and start walking away. He should see you, and turn to follow you. This is a good example of clear body language that your dog will respond to with ease.

EXERCISE 8: LEFT TURN

1 Give the command "Back" with the flat of your left hand on the leash.

2 Use your body and left hand.

3 The dog moves ound.

LEFT TURN

For a left turn, use the command "Back". Put your left hand on thc lcash to stop the dog from going in front of you whilst you make the turn. Turn your body to the left – your left shoulder will dip slightly – this again will be the body language that your dog will notice. Make the turn, then take your left hand off the leash and encourage the dog to keep to the heel position. Praise him and smile.

Reinforce this exercise by using a toy to test the dog's ability to watch your body language. Turn, with a clear body movement, in the direction in which you will throw the toy. Your clear body language will tell him that the toy will be going in that direction.

EXERCISE 9: THE RIGHT ABOUT TURN

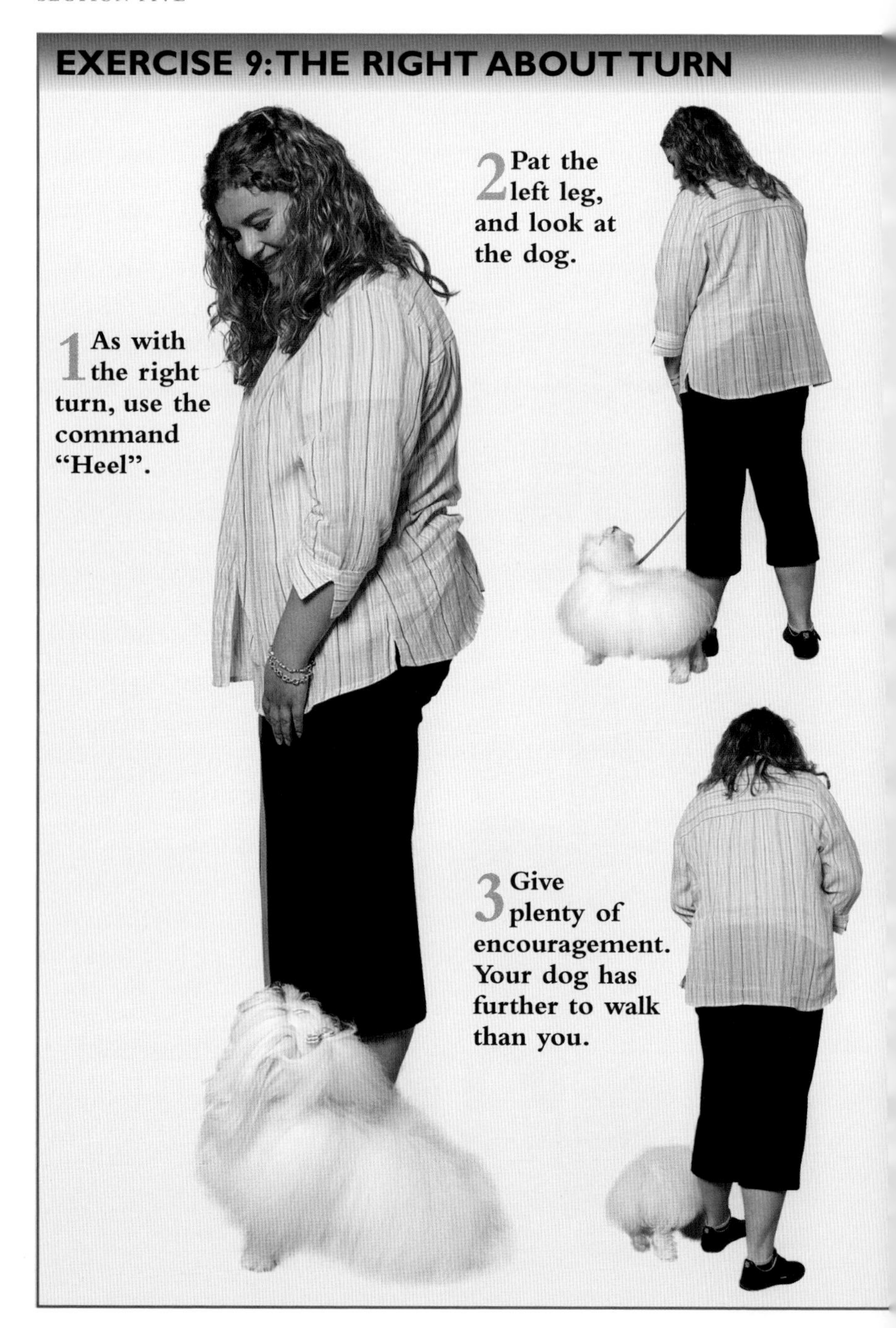

1 As with the right turn, use the command "Heel".

2 Pat the left leg, and look at the dog.

3 Give plenty of encouragement. Your dog has further to walk than you.

4 Smile and praise on completion.

THE RIGHT ABOUT TURN

If you keep walking the same way, you will both get dizzy. To change direction, give the command "Heel" to warn him you are about to change direction. Give a small tug on the leash, and turn your body to the right. Your dog will be familiar with the body language that he has learnt previously for the right turn. Do a complete about-turn to face the opposite direction. Praise as soon as your dog responds.

Reinforce this exercise by occasionally giving no warning. Just change direction. This will encourage the dog to pay extra attention to your body language because suddenly you are no longer at his side. In future he will watch extra carefully for the change in leg movement and the slight dip of your body.

EXERCISE 10: THE LEFT ABOUT TURN

1 Left hand on the leash, give the command "Back".

2 Start making the turn, using clear body language.

3 The dog is almost going backwards.

4 **Praise.**

PACE

Change your walking pace. You may find the word "Steady" helps achieve a slower pace. For a fast pace, increase your speed gradually to a jog. At this speed dogs can get excited, so don't rush it. If he does start jumping up out of excitement, then slow back down, regain control and do more practice at a normal pace.

THE LEFT ABOUT TURN

This turn is the hardest. Turn your body to the left and give the "Back" command. With your left hand on the leash, make the turn. If you have already practiced left turns, the left about turn will be easier to achieve as your dog will read your body language: it is really only a double left turn. Praise, smile and encourage your dog to stay to heel.

The commands suggested above are only guides: if you feel happier using different words, that is fine, as long as you are consistent. Your body language should feel natural when walking: the more relaxed you are, the more your dog will be too.

These turns are essential if you wish to progress to agility training and clear vocal commands will help your dog when he cannot see your body language.

CIRCLING THE DOG DURING HEEL WORK

This is another exercise to keep a dog alert whilst doing heelwork.

Stop, make your dog either sit, lie down or stand still. Tell him to stay. Give the appropriate hand signal, keep your body upright and maintain that hand signal. Walk off with the right leg. Circle him – you may have to repeat the vocal command while you walk round until he has got used to this. If he is sitting, then the command is "Sit, Stay". Repeat both to help him understand. When you return to the heel position, praise, and continue with heelwork. Do this in all three positions: sit, down and stand. At first, do not make the circle too wide. If he turns with you, then just do a half circle to start with, then build it up gradually. Your body language should be upright and confident, and it is important not to lean over your dog. You must look at him throughout this exercise: your head and body will turn naturally. Once you have practised using the vocal commands combined with this body language, you will be able to stop using your voice – your body language alone will be understood. If you are hesitant when you first try this, your negative body language will make your dog unsure. Try it when your dog is confident with you circling him, drop the voice and just try the hand and body actions.

TOY DOGS

Don't let the tiny stature of these dogs fool you – they are often extremely tough and resilient. Toy dogs tend to be intelligent: they read and respond to body language easily. They like to have company and to be kept busy, and perhaps their favourite place is an empty lap. Well-known breeds in this group include the Pekingese (puppies pictured below) and Poodle; less common are the Toy Fox Terrier and the Havanese.

EXERCISE 11: CIRCLING THE DOG IN THE SIT

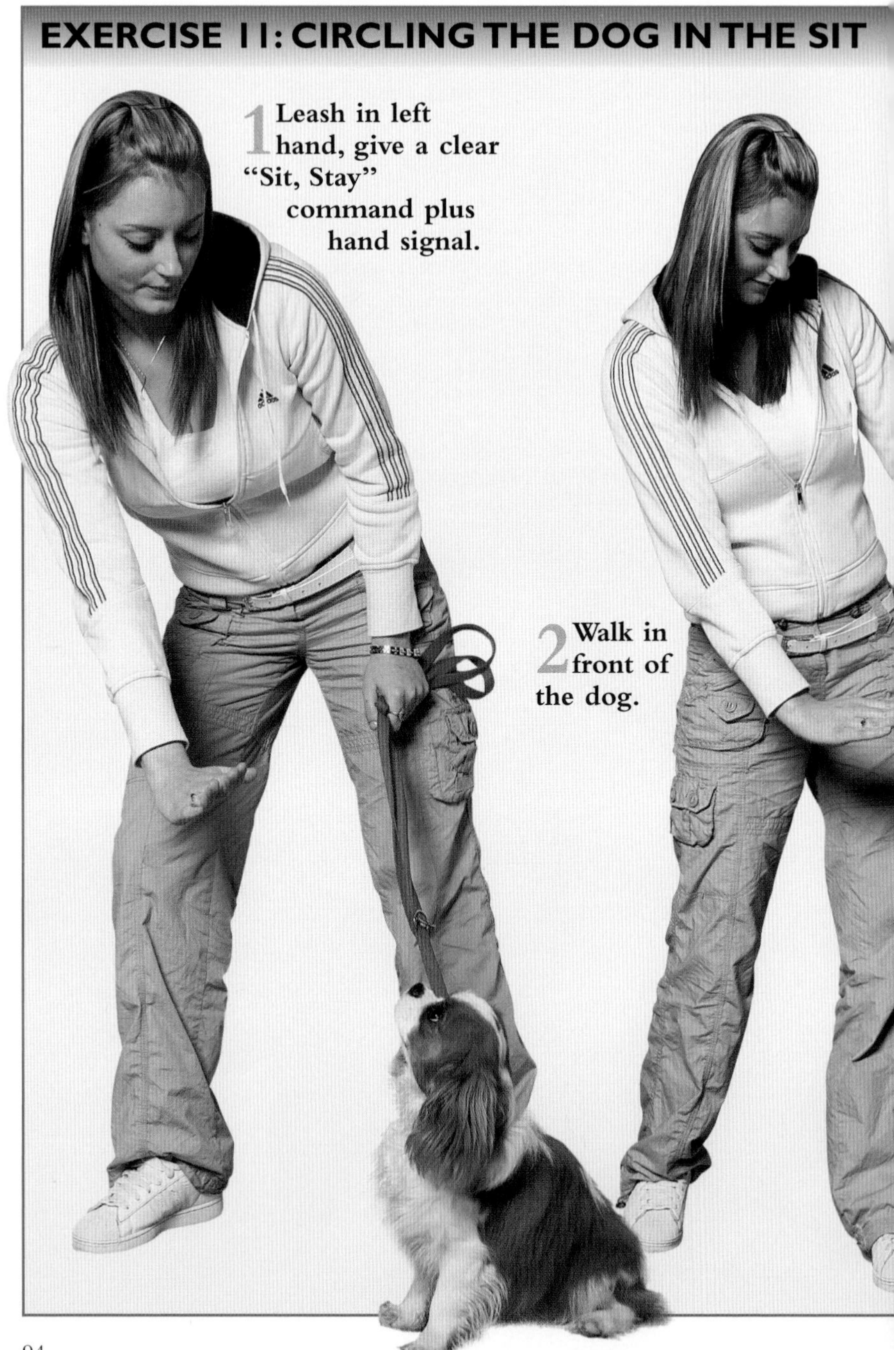

1 Leash in left hand, give a clear "Sit, Stay" command plus hand signal.

2 Walk in front of the dog.

3 Note the position of the hand signal: higher for the sit.

4 As you get round the back of the dog, give an extra vocal command "Sit, Stay."

5 Praise, transfer the leash and continue with heel work.

EXERCISE 12: CIRCLING THE DOG IN THE STAND

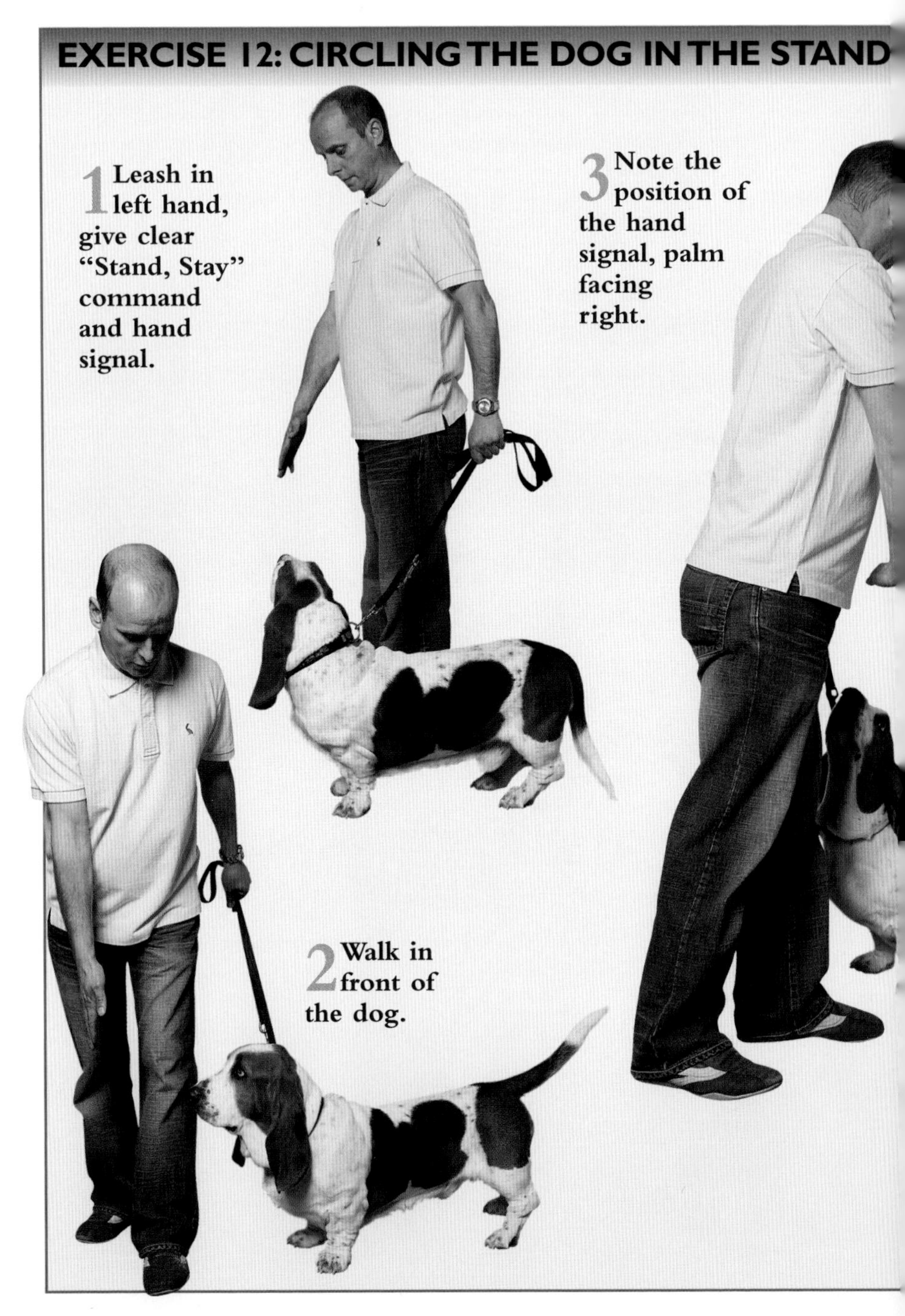

1 Leash in left hand, give clear "Stand, Stay" command and hand signal.

2 Walk in front of the dog.

3 Note the position of the hand signal, palm facing right.

4 As you get round the back, give an extra vocal command: "Stand, Stay."

5 Praise, transfer the leash and continue with the heel work.

EXERCISE 13: CIRCLING THE DOG IN THE DOWN

1 Leash in left hand, give a clear "Down, Stay" command and hand signal.

2 Walk in front of the dog.

3 Note the position of the hand signal, hand facing downwards.

5 Praise, transfer the leash and continue with the heel work.

4 As you get round the back of the dog, give an extra vocal command: "Down, Stay."

THE RECALL

This exercise is about getting your dog back to you, regardless of what he is doing. Your body language should be at its most welcoming for the recall – you must have a happy face and use an excited voice.

For motivation you should use either two treats or a toy. Start with the dog on the leash in the sit position on your left. Give the vocal command "Stay", and a clear high hand stay signal. Walk off with your right leg. Maintain the stay command and the hand signal while you go to the end of the leash. Face your dog, and keep your feet slightly apart. Dogs cannot see as clearly as humans, so give a clear hand signal that your dog will be able to see from a distance. Your body language should look a lot like the letter "T". Stretch out your arms and give the command "Come" with a really welcoming expression on your face. Give a gentle tug on the leash, moving your hands down the leash to take up the slack. At the same time, encourage him with your voice until he is directly in front of you, almost touching your legs. If you lean forward, you will push him away from you. The further away from you he sits, the more distractions he will be able to see. Give the command "Sit". Release the treat and praise, but keep the dog in the sit position.

After a few attempts, you should not have to give the tug on the leash: your dog should come to you happily. The first few times you try this exercise off the leash, only go the same distance that you did with your dog on the leash. You can increase the distance from which you call him by taking a couple of extra steps before you turn to face him.

TERRIERS

Terriers are known for their feisty characters and high energy levels. They were originally bred to hunt vermin, and reveal their natural speed and dexterity when doing agility exercises. They are not always tolerant of other dogs, and you must have great determination to be in full control of a terrier. Well-known terrier breeds include the Airedale (pictured below) and the Jack Russell; less common are the Lakeland and the Kerry Blue. These Airedale Terriers are tethered with slip collars, which I do not recommend - they can be unsafe. Use normal collars for tethering.

EXERCISE 14: THE RECALL PART 1

1 Have your two treats ready in your hand. Leash in the left hand – not too long a leash.

2 A clear 'Sit, Stay' signal.

3 **Look over your left shoulder to ensure you never lose sight of your dog. Use the 'Stay' signal.**

4 **As soon as you move your hand, your dog will be ready to come to you.**

EXERCISE 14: THE RECALL PART 2

5 The voice command should be encouraging.

6 Guide the dog in, holding the treats in the centre of your legs.

7 Hands up, not too high or the dog will jump up. A sharp "Sit" command.

8 Give a treat and praise.

THE FINISH

Your dog is sitting in front of you having just achieved the recall. He has been given a treat and is awaiting the next command. You need to get him into the heel position so he will be ready to set off doing heelwork or continuing your walk. This is the 'finish'.

Pass the leash behind your back from right to left. Give the command "Heel". Move your right leg back to help your dog. With your right hand holding the treat or toy, encourage him to go behind you. When he is right behind you, bring your right leg back, level with the other one. Turn your head to the left and look over your shoulder at him. Bring your right arm back to the front of your body. With this arm, hold the treat near to his nose. Encourage him to come to heel. When his shoulder is level with your leg, give the "Sit" command and praise. Give a treat, or have a break and play with a toy.

The recall and finish are treated as two separate exercises for a reason. If your dog is returning to you, it is better that he focuses on your face rather than on going behind you for the heel position. In time, he will be coming towards you at speed, and if he focuses on going behind you then he may get distracted – perhaps spotting another dog in the distance and deciding to go and play.

Show how pleased you are that he has come to you. Make sure your body language is relaxed, have a happy face and use an excitable voice. You should use all three assets.

TIP

Your head automatically turns to the right to encourage him in the first stage. When your dog has mastered the Finish, just a flick of the head and hand will be all the body language needed.

MISCELLANEOUS BREEDS

This is a varied group, consisting of the less common breeds (and not to be confused with the crossbreeds, see page 135). Most are large dogs, with guarding and herding instincts, and a good ability to read body language. Pictured below is the Dogue de Bordeaux (wearing a choke chain, which I do not recommend – see page 19). Other breeds in this group include the Tibetan Mastiff and the Beauceron.

EXERCISE 15: THE FINISH

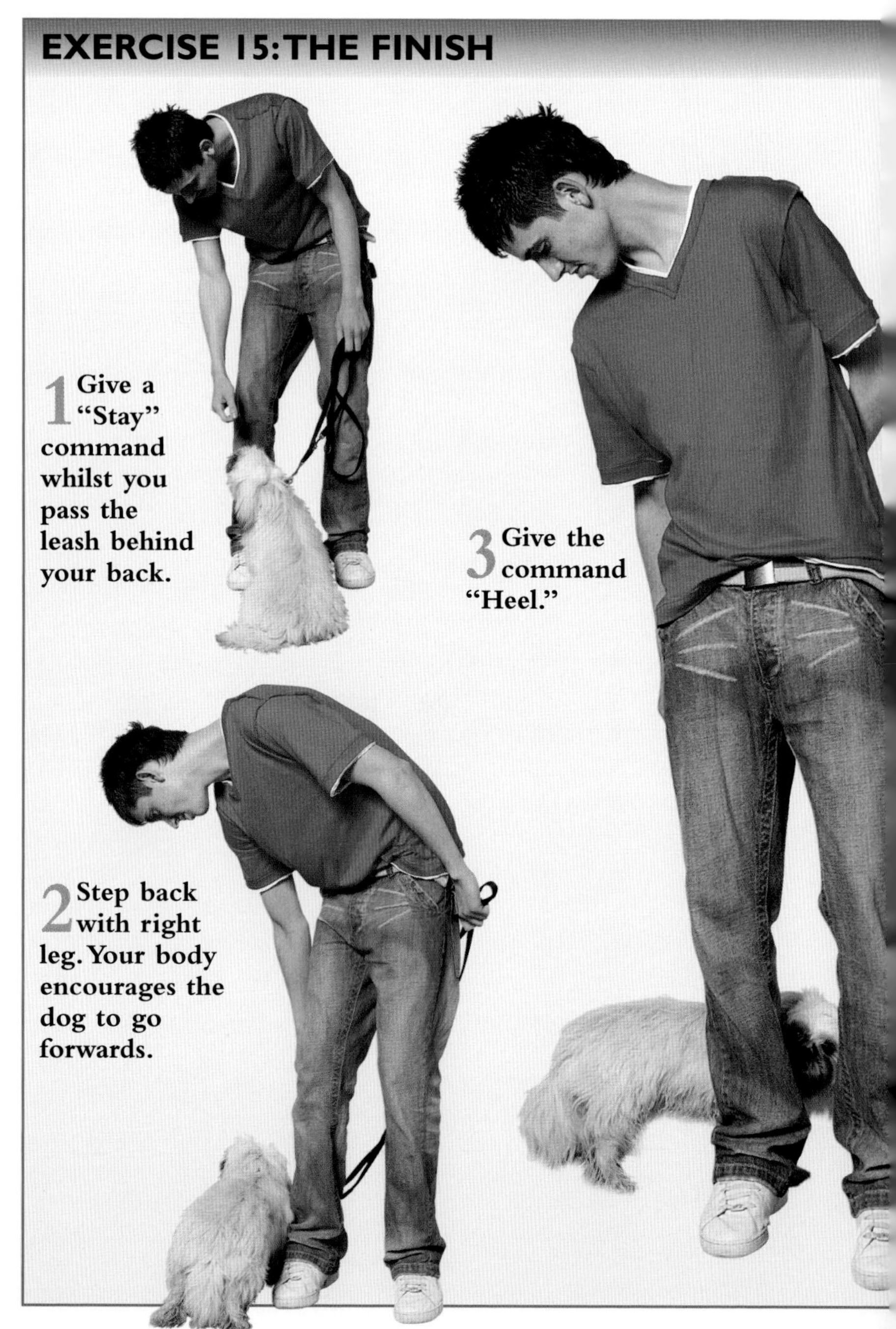

1 Give a "Stay" command whilst you pass the leash behind your back.

2 Step back with right leg. Your body encourages the dog to go forwards.

3 Give the command "Heel."

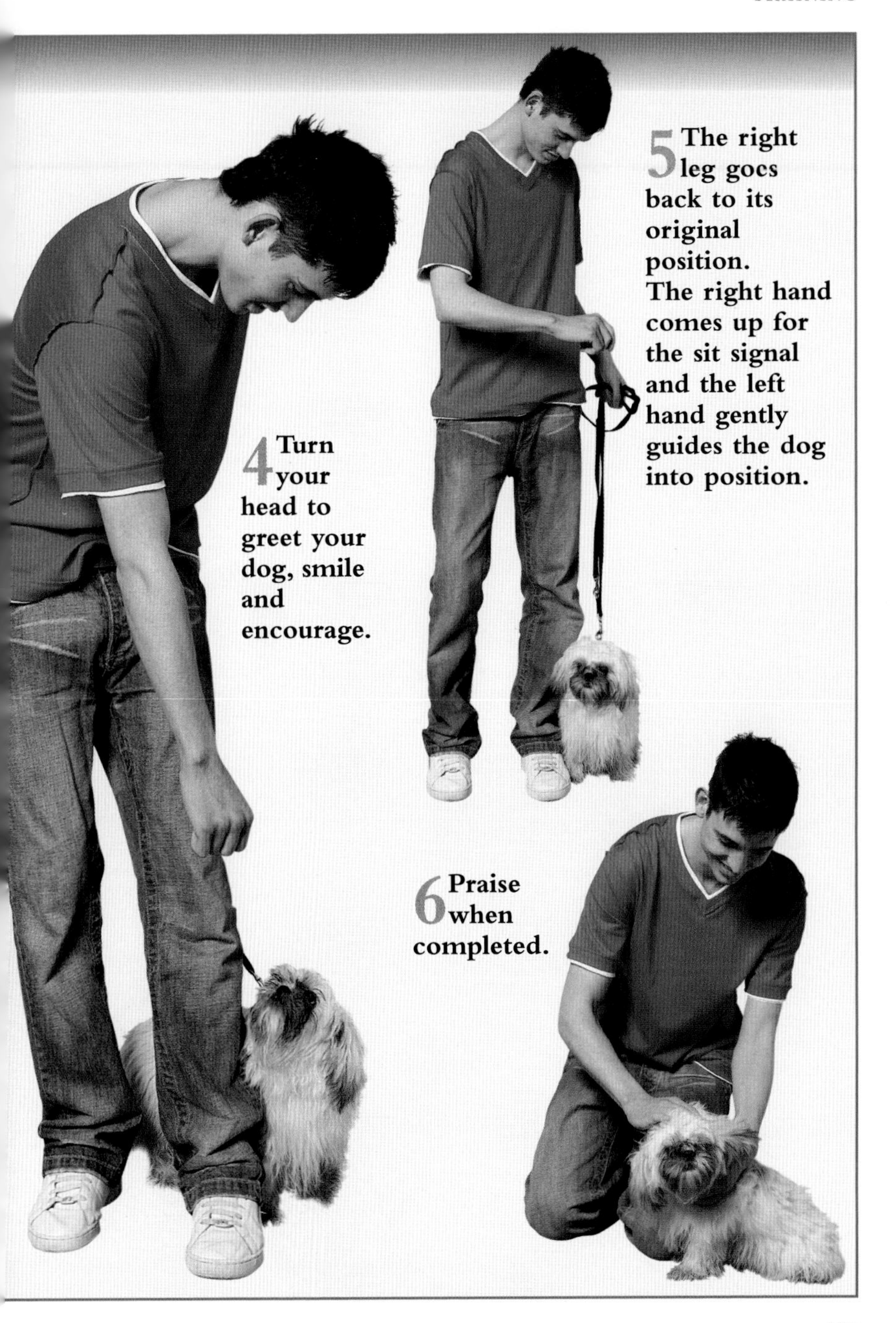

4 Turn your head to greet your dog, smile and encourage.

5 The right leg goes back to its original position. The right hand comes up for the sit signal and the left hand gently guides the dog into position.

6 Praise when completed.

EXERCISE 16: FULL RECALL WITH FINISH PAR

1 This is the first stage of a controlled recall off the leash. Calling your dog to you in a training session reminds him that whenever you call he should respond instantly to you. Good stay needed, nice upright body.

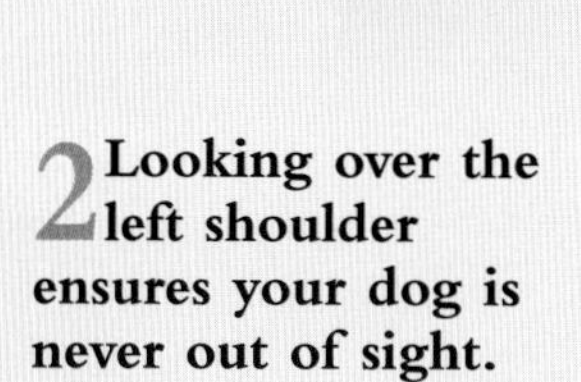

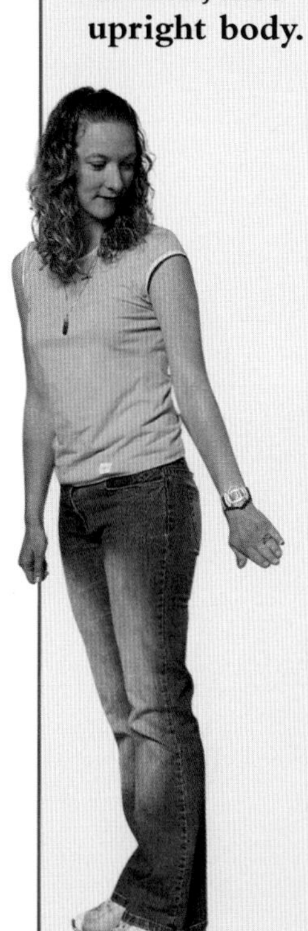

2 Looking over the left shoulder ensures your dog is never out of sight.

3 **Clear long distance hand signals can be seen easily by the dog. The body language is inviting, and if your dog is close enough and is watching you, you will not need to use vocal commands.**

4 **Once your dog is trained on the leash, with practice any distance can be achieved.**

From a distance your body (left) should make an obvious T shape when you start calling.

EXERCISE 16: FULL RECALL WITH FINISH PART

6 **Hands central for the sit and reward. Even with a small dog, keep an upright position rather than a stoop, which will only push your dog away.**

5 **A good straight line with the body and the dog then, with the hands, guide the dog into position.**

7 Give a clear signal to help the dog back to heel position.

8 Encourage with the voice, and smile. Mission accomplished.

EXERCISE 17: THE LEFT FINISH

1 Flat of the left hand on the leash.

2 Give the command "Side." Left leg goes back.

3 Help the dog to go round in an anticlockwise direction, using clear body signals. Allow enough room for your dog to turn by making sure that the leash is not too tight, and that you arm can stretch enough for your dog to be able to do a complet circle comfortably.

4 The right hand comes up for the sit signal and the left hand gently guides the dog into position.

5 Praise on completion.

THE LEFT FINISH

Teaching the left finish will avoid your dog anticipating, when he comes to you in a recall, trotting round to the heel position without been commanded to do so. If he does this, then he is not really paying attention and could easily get distracted.

With your dog sitting in front of you, hold the leash in the right hand. Put your left hand on the leash, close to him. Give the command "Side" and lean back slightly. Use your hand to gently pull the leash to bring the dog anticlockwise into the heel position. Give the command "Sit", then praise him. Again, a flick of the left hand or a tilt of the head will eventually be all the body language you will need for this exercise.

DISTANCE CONTROL

Distance control teaches you to command your dog from a distance without him moving forward. If your dog had escaped and was the other side of a road, for example, you would not want him to cross the road to get back to you. With distance control, you could command him to stay until it was safe for you to cross the road to collect him. Distance control could save your dog's life.

THE DOWN

Put your dog in the sit. Stand about three feet away, facing him. Use clear, confident hand signals and body language. Step forward with the right leg only. With your right arm, point your hand to the floor. Bend your body forwards and give the command "Down". Release a treat and praise. Move your leg back.

THE STAND

To make him stand, step forward with the right leg. Give the command "Stand". Move your hand with the treat towards the dog's mouth. Lean back and gradually bring your hand back until the dog is standing. Release the treat and praise him.

THE SIT

For a sit, again step forwards with the right leg. Raise your right arm and give the command "Sit".

When you practise these exercises, change the order of commands, and don't rush. It is important not to try to increase the distance between you and your dog until he is responding to your first command, and is not moving forwards. Distance control takes time to teach, and if your dog does start to move forwards when you try to go further away, then go back closer to him and start again. Only do the sit, stand and down a couple of times each, or you will bore your dog.

WORKING DOGS

These dogs are strong – training them well is essential because an unruly, powerful dog can be dangerous. (Of all the breeds it is perhaps most highly recommended that you take a working dog to a training school.) They are intelligent, quick to pick up body language, and make excellent guard dogs. Some of the breeds are used for pulling sledges and water rescue. Well-known working dog breeds include the Saint Bernard (pictured above) and the Great Dane. Less common are the Siberian Husky and Tibetan Mastiff.

EXERCISE 18: DISTANCE CONTROL/DOWN

1 Leash in left hand. Right hand giving the 'Down' signal. Right leg forward, voice command "Down."

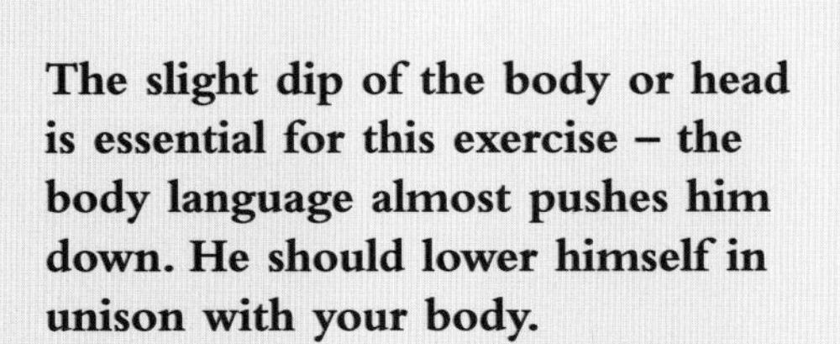

The slight dip of the body or head is essential for this exercise – the body language almost pushes him down. He should lower himself in unison with your body.

2 Use facial expression, voice and body language.

3 Step back, but don't over praise, or your dog may get up.

EXERCISE 19: DISTANCE CONTROL/STAND

1 Give the command "Stand". Gently pull the leash. Right hand signal. Lean backwards.

2 Palm facing right.

3 After you have brought your leg back, maintain the voice and hand signal as the dog will be tempted to move forwards.

EXERCISE 20: DISTANCE CONTROL/SIT

1 Right foot forwards to encourage the dog almost to go backwards. Note the bent knee.

2 High hand signal

3 Maintain the hand signal and voice if needed.

Your body language should be upright for this manoeuvre, and the hand signal should be high. Once the dog is looking upwards, it will be easier for him to focus on you.

EXERCISE 21: DISTANCE CONTROL OFF LEASH

1 Once mastered, the dog will stay in position for all three commands.

The further away you are from your dog in this exercise, the harder it will be for him to read your facial expression. All the more important to give clear signals from the body.

2 In time, one signal will be enough: either the body, the voice or just the hand.

3 In time you should be able to do distance control from several metres away using just body language and hand signals.

RETRIEVE

The retrieve is a fun exercise, but, as always, it is crucial that you are in control.

Use a toy that does not roll when you throw it (or your dog may push it further away, hoping to start a game). He probably loves balls, and if you must use one, buy one attached to a rope (which is less easy for him to push along). If he is excited and strains to get to the toy, be careful not to chastise him, or you may put him off the exercise.

As with all other exercises, train initially on the leash. With your dog on your left, give the command "Stay". Throw the toy or a dumbell (a dumbell is shown on page 19) just a few feet in front of you. Give the command "Fetch", and move your left leg forwards towards the toy. Your dog has to go round your leg to get to it. Let him go to pick it up. He will then be facing you: call him to you using the command "Come". When he does, praise him. (If he tries to run off with the article rather than come to you, give a gentle tug on the leash to get him back.) Move backwards yourself, as with the puppy recall (see page 72), encouraging him to come to you. Give the command "Sit." Praise him, but don't snatch the toy from him. Give the command "Leave", put your hand in front of his face with your fingers apart, facing upwards and towards him. Take the article away from him and give praise.

TIP

When you are satisfied that your dog is happy with the exercise and completes it well, you can do a Finish as a finale. Once your dog is retrieving and coming back willingly, you can progress to doing this exercise off the leash.

GUARD BREEDS

There is no specific Kennel Club guard group classification; instead, guard breeds consist of various breeds from other groups. Despite negative publicity about guard dogs such as Rottweilers, Dobermans and German Shepherds, these breeds are highly intelligent. Correct training is essential and they need plenty of stimulus and exercise: give them this, and they'll adapt to family life. They are extremely protective by nature. Guard dogs are often used for police work and for mountain or other types of rescue.

EXERCISE 22: RETRIEVING ON LEASH PART 1

1 Keep the leash slack to avoid giving the dog a jerk on the neck that could put him off fetching the toy.

2 Hold on to the collar while you throw the article.

3 Blocking the toy with your left leg means that the dog has to go round your leg and ends up facing you. This way he will also find it difficult to knock the toy further away from you and create a new game.

4 He is more likely to come to you now he is facing you.

EXERCISE 22: RETRIEVING ON LEASH PART 2

5 Hold the toy gently so as not to start a pulling game.

6 Fingers spread for the 'Leave' command.

7 Playing afterwards is a good enough reward.

Don't use too long a leash for this exercise: if he gets caught up in it he may be put off retrieving.

EXERCISE 23: RETRIEVING OFF LEASH

1 Off the leash and in control – both handler and dog look happy.

2 A dog happy to retrieve.

3 **The result.**

A retrieve is virtually the same as a recall (page 100) once your dog has picked up the object. So, use the same body language as you would when you call your dog – arms clearly outstretched as soon as he turns to face you.

TREATS

I find certain types of treat particularly useful in my school. Some are more practical than others. For example, treats that break up easily are rather unfair, since those dogs which haven't been rewarded can still come sniffing round for the crumbs. Dried tripe, liver or small biscuits are better. Or you can make your own, perhaps for use only when training, so it becomes special. Keep treats in an easily accessible pocket – if you have to open a bag and fiddle around, your dog will forget what he did to deserve his reward.

LIVERCAKE RECIPE

INGREDIENTS

12 oz (340 gm) fresh liver
12 oz (340 gm) plain flour
(can use gluten free flour)
1 large egg
1-2 cloves of garlic, crushed
(or ½ - 1 teaspoon
dried garlic granules.)
Milk or water to mix

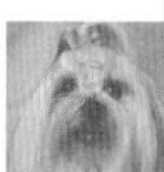

Liquidize the liver, egg and crushed garlic (this is easiest if the liver is cut into small pieces).

Add the dried garlic to the flour.

Add enough milk or water to make approximately 3/4 pint (0.5 litre). If using gluten-free flour, you may need an extra couple of tablespoons.

Add the liver mix to the flour, and mix well until it has a cake consistency.

Pour into two 9-inch (225-mm), well-greased cake tins or similar.

Bake at 325°F (160°C) for about 30 to 40 minutes, until firm to the touch.

Leave to cool for ten minutes, turn out and then cut into cubes.

CROSSBREEDS

Not to be confused with the miscellaneous group (see page 107), crossbreeds can either be a straight cross between two breeds (and possess traits of each), or can have a parentage of several breeds that goes back generations. As a result, crossbreeds tend to be hardy, and are often used for rescue work. Inevitably, every crossbreed is an individual – and it can take patience to train them. The results, however, are usually rewarding. Although not recognised by the Kennel Club, there are many shows purely for crossbreeds.

SOLVING TRAINING PROBLEMS

MY DOG WON'T RETRIEVE

A dog that shows no interest in retrieving needs to be taught how to play, and this can take a long time. You need to find something that interests him. If he is a rescue dog, then he has probably been told off for picking things up, or has simply never had the opportunity to play.

Try stuffing a sock with his favourite treats, attaching it to a string and encouraging him to chase it. If he picks it up, praise him and reward with a treat. Finding something he really likes to play with may not be easy. Watch him for a while, and take note of what

interests him. Is it a ball? An old gardening glove? Use something that is easy to pick up – it may take trial and error to find the one that suits him best. If he likes fabric more than plastic, go for a material that absorbs least saliva: a dry mouth is uncomfortable.

Make the training fun.

Pretending to throw, teasing your dog with the toy, can help get him excited, keen to fetch the toy.

MY DOG WON'T HOLD ON TO THE RETRIEVED ARTICLE

If your dog drops the retrieved toy as soon as he gets to you, this may be happening for one of two reasons.

Reason one. When teaching him to retrieve, you have always picked up the toy as soon as he has dropped it at your feet. You have then thrown it for him straight away, and he has learnt that this is the order of the exercise. To get him to hold on to the toy, use a ball on a rope. Rather than throwing it, play having a tug of war with him. Smile lots, and laugh with him. When he is excited, give the "Sit" command. Don't let go of the toy, but don't play at tugging any more either. Your body language should change and become upright, so he realises the game is over. Give the command "Hold" in a soft voice, followed immediately by praise. After a couple of seconds, give the "Leave" command, and take the toy. Give the release command "OK", and start to tease him again with the toy. Throw it for him, and, as he comes back to you, turn away from him. This should make him come closer. If he has not dropped the toy, then start the play tugging again.

If he has dropped the toy, try to encourage him to pick it up by grabbing the rope and dragging it along. Give the command "Hold" in a happy tone. In time, and with

practice, your dog should start bringing the toy back to you so you can play with it together. He wants to enjoy fetching, but remember every dog is different: some will cotton on faster than others. Persevere, and have fun at the same time.

Reason two. The toy might have been snatched out of your dog's mouth when he has retrieved in the past - not a pleasant experience. Fearing a repeat of this, he prefers to drop the toy for you.

Treat him to a new toy, perhaps a soft one would be best. Throw it for him, and

If you have an energetic dog, start by throwing the toy a good distance and run in the opposite direction to get him to chase you. As soon as he is level with you, try to grab the toy and play tug.

as he is returning with it, walk away from him. Use a soft, but commanding voice, and keep your body language upright. Call him to heel, praising when he responds. As you are walking with him in the heel position, look at him and tell him he is a good boy, and gently give the command "Hold". If you quicken your pace, he will be less likely to drop the toy. After a few steps, stop. Give the "Sit" command. Step in front of him, facing him. Put your hands under his chin and raise his head slightly. Give kind, soothing praise, with intermittent "Hold" commands. With his head slightly raised it will be harder

This is the Collie's favourite position – his body language is poised and alert, and he is ready to play.

for him to drop the toy. After a couple of seconds, very gently give the vocal command "Leave", together with the leave hand signal. Take the toy from him. Now give him plenty of praise. You may have to do this several times before he brings the toy directly to you.

ARMCHAIR FETCH

This is a useful training exercise for a wet day. Sitting in an armchair, throw the toy. When he picks it up, use the recall signal (page 100). Have your hands cupped in your lap to show that you want to receive it there. After a few tries, cup your hands out in front. If he drops the toy, don't bend down to pick it up. Pat your lap to signal that this is where you want him to drop it.

MY DOG WON'T LEAVE THE RETRIEVED TOY

Make him sit in front of you. Hold the leash close to his collar, and very gently hold the toy – not pulling or tugging it as this encourages him to play. Firmly give the command "Leave", and wait for him to release it. You may have to wait a long time. If this doesn't work after a while, try offering him a treat, praising him when he releases the toy. Alternatively, put him on a leash, make him sit, and give the "Stay" command. Put his favourite toy in front of him. Give the hand and voice signal for the leave command. If he pulls towards the toy, gently pull him back and say "Leave" until he loses interest.

The "leave" command with the palm of the hand facing the dog, fingers splayed open.

Gently does it. No snatching the toy away from your dog

MY DOG WON'T CONCENTRATE IN CLASS

Often enough, the solution to this problem is to keep special treats which you use just for training (see page 134). However, it is important also to ascertain whether you are giving your dog enough praise. Are you focusing on him, or looking around at the

A good example of both dog and handler concentrating on each other

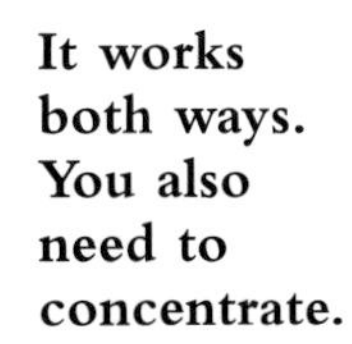

It works both ways. You also need to concentrate.

others? Is he bored? Perhaps try playing with a toy in between exercises. Another suggestion is to give him more hands-on attention in class and less at home. Whenever he looks at you, praise him so as to reinforce your bond. Take him outside and play with him one to one. Turn suddenly away from him, and reward him when he follows.

If you find that you get results at home but not at school, ask your instructor for advice as to where you could be going wrong.

With time, patience and bonding you too can achieve this.

MY DOG IS AGGRESSIVE TO OTHER DOGS

Dominance aggression. If your dog without warning one day starts this behaviour, then it could well be hormonal – the teenage years. When he shows aggression to another dog, be firm with him, and show strong disapproval in your facial body language. Use the command "Leave." Turn him towards you to get his attention. As soon as he responds, reward him with a treat and show

Using a head collar will make you feel more confident, as it gives you control over his head rather than just his neck.

The handlers have confident body language, and their leashes are not too long or too tight, enabling the dogs to greet each other but still be kept under control.

him a happy face. Talk using a high-pitched, happy voice. Tell him how lovely the other dog is. While he may not understand what you are saying, he will pick up positive vibrations from you.

Is your dog aggressive because he's trying to be macho? Does he show off to bitches? Does he consider all male dogs a threat? Castration could be the answer, but it will not solve the aggression entirely. (For castration to have maximum benefit it needs to be done before the dog is 12 months old. Castrating an older dog can still be effective, but the

younger it is done the better.) Castration takes away sexual frustration, which is often the cause of dog fights. See page 164 for more information about castration.

Are you the pack leader at home? If not, he might be aggressive because he is trying to protect you. Re-read the advice in section 3.

If he persists in grabbing others and biting, it may be necessary to use a muzzle. Be aware: if he needs a muzzle, then he also needs to stay on his leash.

A Halti-type head collar will give you more control, especially if you have a big dog. Try not to tighten the leash when you see another dog, as this alerts him to the possibility of there being a problem, and puts him on edge. Be as relaxed as you can: show it in your body language.

The handlers are distracting the dogs from each other, and rewarding their unaggressive behaviour with a treat.

Nervous aggression. Your dog may be defensive because he has been attacked by other dogs, or perhaps he was not socialized from an early age. A common sign of nervous aggression is raised hair on the back, and ears lowered. He may feel especially vulnerable in a room where he can see no obvious exit. Once again, you must be a confident pack leader, and reassure him that nothing bad will happen to him.

If your dog constantly barks at the other dogs in the class, then it may be best to stop group sessions and have a one-to-one with the instructor. This might well be less stressful for you both. If you cannot arrange this, try playing with toys to distract him – such as a ball on a rope. Make this toy special: one that you use just for training.

Work hard at having fun after each completed

Dogs pick up friendly body language and tone of voice from their owners, and relax into chance meeting situations such as this.

exercise. This will get him interested. If you have a rescue dog and he doesn't know how to play, use extra treats. Practice at home with different toys and teach him how to play. Use plenty of rewards when you encounter other dogs, so that your dog expects a treat when he sees another dog.

It often calms a dog down if you make him sit and look at you. Have calm, confident body language. Never shout – use a soft voice. If you find you have to use many treats to improve his neurotic behaviour, then remember to cut down his food – you don't want a fat dog.

Make sure your dog spends time with dogs of the opposite sex, as they pose less of a threat. Perhaps try to find someone who owns a friendly, confident dog of the opposite sex, and take them for walks together. The more he socializes, the better.

MY DOG IS AGGRESSIVE TO PEOPLE

If your dog shows aggression as people are walking towards you, give the command "Leave"; gain control and make him sit. If possible, distract him with a favourite treat, and praise if he responds by taking it. Make sure you

This is not acceptable behaviour. Ignoring this problem will not make it go away.

tell people to ignore him, by not looking at him or touching him. He will gain confidence, and will stop being aggressive as he learns that they pose no threat.

Curing this problem is all about being in full control, so do this training on the leash in a public place. You must be especially well tuned to his body language, and must watch out for any changes in him that may signal the approach of people. Forewarned is forearmed.

Once he becomes more relaxed when strangers approach, get someone he knows fairly well to hold a treat in their hand, while not looking at him. When he takes it, they should praise him gently, but still avoid eye contact. Do not rush this: you must have patience. Some dogs can take a long time to gain confidence with people. You might meet dog 'experts' who tell you that this is bad advice; that the way to deal with an aggressive dog is to lean over him and speak soothingly. Don't listen to them: leaning over a dog comes across as threatening body language. Dogs threatened in this way may lunge at people, who will then tell you what a nasty dog you have. Avoid these 'experts', or ask them to ignore your dog. Otherwise they risk undoing all your good work.

If your dog is relaxed with other dogs, then go for walks with several other dog owners and their dogs to get him used to people as well. My own dog, Soni, was very aggressive to people, having been beaten and abandoned. He had two options: either to be put to sleep, or live in a rescue kennel. Now he is great with people. It simply took time and patience applying these simple principles.

Occasionally, due to inbred aggressive traits, or through a lack of early socialization, a dog will not respond. If you feel your dog falls into this category, see a behaviourist or a dog psychologist. Get a second opinion, and a third. Maybe you will have to make a hard decision. Do you want to live with a permanently muzzled dog?

If you do need to use a muzzle, choose one carefully. I prefer basket muzzles as they allow the dog to pant, drink and eat treats whilst still preventing him from biting.

When your dog is muzzled you may find other dog owners give you a wide berth. It is important to maintain confident and calm body language with your dog in these situations, especially if you want your dog to get used to people and other dogs. Don’t get excited trying to explain to people why your dog is muzzled – approach in a calm manner, with your dog under control. Dog owners will often respond positively if they see that you are training your dog to behave.

This dog is learning that she does not have to defend herself against people.

MY DOG CHASES LIVESTOCK

If your dog chases livestock, not only is this upsetting and frightening for the animals, but it is also dangerous for him, as a farmer may shoot him. My best solution to this problem is to make a distraction can. This is very simple: get an empty drink can and put small pebbles inside. Put your dog on a leash and take him close to livestock, but not in the same field. Your body language should be relaxed. When your dog starts to show too much interest in

Training with a distraction can is best done behind a fence.

A dog can easily be trained by a wheelchair user with upper body language and voice. Dogs are often not given credit for how adaptable they are.

the livestock, say "Leave" firmly. Maintain a confident stance and a stern expression. If he ignores you, throw the can to the ground so it makes as much noise as possible. This should spook him. Pick the can up, and put it back in your pocket. Even though your dog is on the leash, give the hand signal for 'come', along with a vocal command. Your body language should now be welcoming. If he does not respond, give a quick tug on the leash. When he does come to you, give him plenty of praise. Use the can again as soon as he starts showing too much interest in the livestock. Praise him when he shows no more interest.

MY DOG PINCHES FOOD OFF THE WORK SURFACE

Put some food on a work surface and take your dog into the kitchen on the leash. If he goes for the food, say "Leave". If he responds, bring him towards you and give praise. It will take more than one go at this to stop this problem. If he pinches food only when you are out of the room, then set up a trap. Put some tins on a tray (no sharp edges) and balance this on the edge of a work surface. Put some treats on the part of the tray that is overhanging. When your dog jumps up, as he pinches the treat, the noise of the tins crashing down should be enough to stop him doing it again. If not, go back to the technique described above.

A dog has to learn that just because food is on the floor, it does not mean that it is for him.

MY DOG BARKS CONSTANTLY AT THE WINDOW

If your dog jumps onto a chair to look out of the window, you should move the chair in order to break the cycle. Have you been shouting at your dog to stop him barking? If so, he may think you are joining in. Keep your voice low, and call him to you. If he doesn't respond, slam a distraction can on to the floor (see chasing livestock, page 156). This problem usually arises when a dog lacks exercise and mental stimulation.

I'm shouting at you.

MY DOG IS LIVELY ALL THE TIME

Firstly, check that the food you are giving him is not for working dogs – as only these dogs need this type of food. If you are giving a feed with additives, these could be affecting him. Wheat can also affect dogs: I have seen aggression disappear with several dogs when wheat was removed from their diet.

Is your dog getting enough exercise? There are 24 hours in a day: if your dog only has two hours of walking or playing, can you really expect him to rest for the other 22 hours? Go out in the garden

Playing together is more fun than on your own, and this is ideal bonding time for the pair of you.

and throw toys for a while. Make a couple of jumps, and have some fun with him. Hide a toy and watch him find it. Dogs love to have a run to burn off energy. A toy that has compartments for treats will keep him quieter and busier as he tries to extract the rewards.

Using the nose is so natural for a dog.

A simple but effective jump. Don't make the jump too high, or your dog may go under rather than over.

MY DOG CONSTANTLY BARKS IN THE CAR

Put your dog in the car, and sit in it too, reading the paper. Use your calmest, most relaxed body language. When he has settled, take him back into the house. Repeat this several times. Once he has got used to this, turn the engine on and sit quietly, listening to the radio. Repeat again until he settles.

The next stage involves driving around the block. Simply go around the block in the car – so that he gets into the car at home and doesn't get out until he gets back home, with nothing exciting in between. Make sure he is secure and cannot jump over the seats. If he barks, don't shout: he may think you are joining in. Once he realizes he is not going anywhere exciting, he should settle.

Vary where you take him for exercise. Dogs soon get used to the routes you take in

Going nowhere fast.

the car, and can scent areas they have visited before. The flick of the indicator can also be a signal to your dog that he has arrived at an exciting destination. I know dogs who, when being driven to training school, start crying with excitement as soon as they turn into the lane – even if the owner has tried to fool them by coming a different way.

MOUNTS ANYTHING, INCLUDING THE CHILDREN

As soon as he shows signs of mounting, try distracting him with toys. If this fails, a squirt of water may well cool his ardour. Ask yourself, is he getting enough exercise? If the problem really is severe, you might need to consider castration. Talk to your vet.

For the operation, you normally take your dog into the vet in the morning, and collect him in the afternoon (though this varies). Your dog may have to wear a bucket-type collar to stop him ripping out the stitches, but after 10 days he should be able to resume a normal life. It takes about six weeks before you see results. Castration only takes

'Masculine' breeds still look masculine after castration.

away the sexual urge of the dog, not his energy. It can, however, prevent fights with other dogs because his need to be macho has gone; likewise other dogs don't see him as a threat. A bitch on heat will no longer pose a problem. Some people will tell you that castration will make your dog fat. This is not true: there is one thing that makes dogs fat - food. If your dog starts to put on weight, cut down on his food and give him more exercise. If he has been castrated and persists in mounting, it may be dominance-related. Ask yourself once more: who is the pack leader?

MY DOG GOES MAD WHEN THE PHONE RINGS

Ringing phones are stimulating: they invariably raise the excitement level in your house, and your dog senses this.

Try getting a friend to telephone you, or use your mobile to ring your land line. When the phone rings, do not

Is it for me?

react. Ignore your dog's behaviour, and don't answer it. Repeat this at intervals. When you actually need to answer the phone, ignore your dog and walk calmly to it. Your body language should be very relaxed, and you should answer in a calm voice.

Once the call is finished, keep ignoring your dog, or he may associate the end of a call with a reward, and start getting edgy for you to finish.

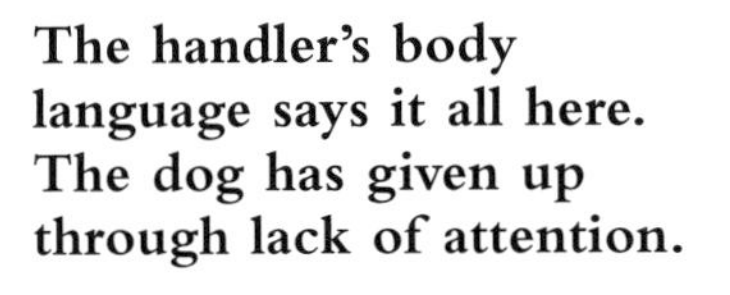

The handler's body language says it all here. The dog has given up through lack of attention.

MY DOG DIGS UP THE GARDEN

Leave activity toys about the garden, such as plastic bottles full of water (which can distract him very efficiently). A large solid ball is also fun, but I know from experience what damage an over-enthusiastic dog can do to plant pots. If you see him digging, give a sharp "No". Call him to you, and reward him when he comes. Then distract him with a toy. You should cut

Use a ball that your dog cannot pick up. He will be able to amuse himself by playing his own version of soccer.

As suggested above, a dog ca[n] help in the garden. When [he is] digging, give th[e] command "Di[g]". Praise him, the[n] give the comm[and] "Leave" and praise. Howeve[r,] don't expect perfect results.

down on the amount of time he is left alone in the garden. It can occasionally be possible to turn this problem to your advantage. See the caption below centre.

A paddling pool is not only cooling, but also great fun. Most dogs love jumping in and out of a small pool. At least they are getting exercise rather than lazing about.

SHOULD I GET MY BITCH SPAYED OR LET HER HAVE A LITTER?

Bitches come into season on average every six months. During this time they can suffer from frustration and the general feeling of being unwell. In fact, they experience symptoms of PMT. If you want her to have a litter, you must ask yourself why. Is it because you want one of her puppies? Supposing she has 12? A responsible breeder should feel able to tell everyone who takes one of the pups that he will

Show dogs such as these Gordon Setters are not spayed. A good show dog will have a waiting list for puppies.

have the pup back if there is a problem. How would you feel if one of your dog's puppies ended up at a rescue centre? The fact is that your bitch will have had enough of her puppies after about six weeks. Can you really guarantee that you will find good homes for them all? Rescue centres are full of unwanted dogs, so think very carefully. Having puppies will not make your bitch a better dog.

Spaying usually involves just one day at the vet. After ten days the stitches can be removed; then she needs light exercise for a few weeks before getting back to normal. Some people think that spaying is cruel, but I really don't believe that to be true. The minor inconvenience of the procedure will soon be forgotten, and once your bitch is spayed several problems are solved for life: no more frustration, no more mess and no more dogs following you around or hanging about the garden for three whole weeks when she comes into season.

ON THE MOVE

IN THE CAR

Obviously, the best way for your dog to travel by car is in a cage, or behind a dog guard – never on the front seat or loose in the car. If you opt for a cage, remember to get one with more than one door. If you had an accident and one door was blocked, then you could let him out through the other.

Take trouble to choose a cage that suits your car and your dog. It needs to be high (and wide) enough to allow your dog to stand up, turn around and lie down comfortably. Most good cages have a side and a front entrance.

If you decide to get a dog guard, make sure that it is easily removable in case of an accident. A front and a rear guard give you extra control when getting a dog out of the

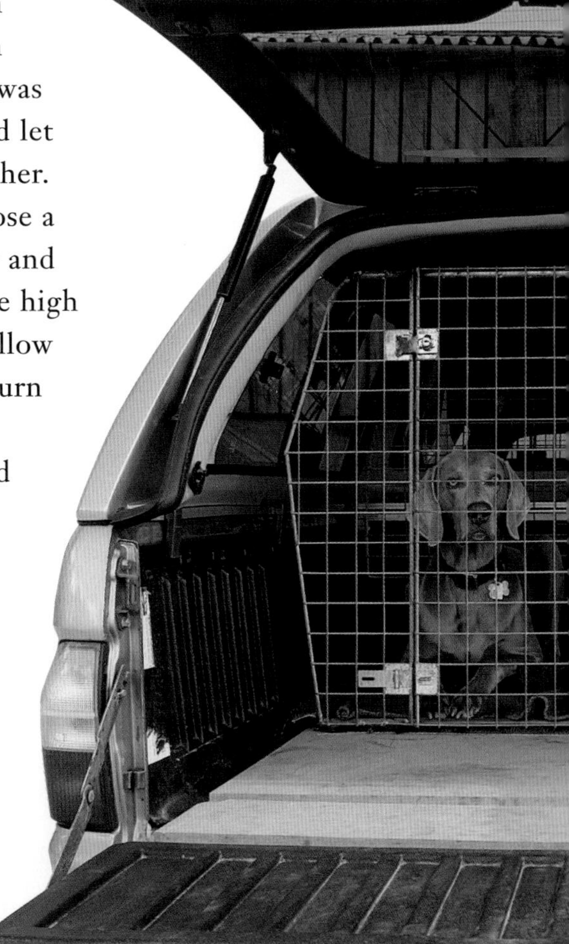

Dogs can feel secure in their mobile kennels. With more than one dog in the family, a cage for each dog provides individual territory.

car: he is prevented from jumping straight out of the back when you open it up. Guards are also useful if you have to leave a dog in the car for any length of time: you can put a lock on the guard and leave the tailgate open to let in fresh air.

DOG TRAVEL BAG

I keep a box or a bag in my car containing:

- Water.
- Bowl.
- Towel.
- First aid kit.
- Spare leash and collar with dog disc.
- Toys.
- Treats.
- A stake for tying up the dog either in an emergency, or where there's no freedom for him to run around.
- A chain to go with the stake: if really frustrated, he could chew through a leather or webbing leash.
- Plastic bags for picking up poo.
- Kitchen roll and disinfectant.

Once assembled, this kit takes up little space and you'll be surprised how useful, even essential, the bag becomes.

If you have to leave your dog in your car make sure, of course, that he will be safe – and that he is locked in.

A trip to the supermarket is not much fun for your dog, so think about whether you really need to take him.

If you don't want to buy a cage or a guard, a car harness will keep your dog physically restricted and safe while you are on the move. Make sure that it fits correctly – and is comfortable (see page 19).

You can also buy special window vents that let plenty of air in, while preventing a dog from poking his nose out of the window. They are reasonably cheap and are easy to fit. Don't let your dog hang his head out of the window as you drive: he may develop ear problems, or be hit by another car passing close. Non-spill bowls, ideal for travelling, are now available.

HOLIDAYS

If you are taking your dog with you on holiday, then preparation is essential. If you are going abroad, be sure to check the regulations: many countries now require a dog to have a passport and injections, to be microchipped and wormed. Passport applications can take up to six months, so you need to visit the vet in good time to get the necessary injections. Your vet will explain all the requirements.

Get a dog tag made with your holiday address and mobile phone number. Find

out before going where the nearest vet will be, and get hold of the phone number. A collapsible cage is useful if you are staying in a hotel: better than coming back to the room after dinner to find that your dog has chewed it up.

If you already have a dog travel bag in the car (see page 173), then add a couple of extra towels, his own bedding, and an old sheet to cover any rugs he may wish to lie on when wet. Also, take a long leash in case it is impossible to let him loose. Some resorts do not allow dogs on the beach – check this before you go.

If you want to eat in a place that does not allow dogs, park the car in a shady place and leave your dog in the car with the tailgate open. If you have a cage or guard, remember to lock this, and make sure that there is fresh water to drink. I never leave my dogs where I can't see them, and often stay by the roadside with the dogs on stakes nearby if it is too hot to stay in the car.

If you are taking two dogs with you on holiday, do some research first – some hotels may only accept one dog.

Purchase a chain or flexible metal line to go with the stake.

Cars in direct sunlight heat up to unbearable temperatures for a dog in just a few minutes. Be aware of this, even if the air temperature is cool. Think of buying windscreen shades or even using a sheet. Caravans also get very hot, so ensure that there is plenty of ventilation and, of course, water.

If your dog gets too hot (it will be obvious from his panting), soak a towel in water and lay it on his back. Don't leave a muzzle on him: he needs to open his mouth fully in order to pant.

KENNELS

If you have to leave your dog behind, the best way to find acceptable kennels is through word of mouth. Make an appointment to visit: don't just drop in unannounced, as constant disruptions are time consuming for kennel staff. Reputable kennels are clean and the dogs look cared for. I prefer kennels that have secure exercise areas with high fences where the dogs can run around. Ask about the security arrangements; in fact, ask as many questions as you can. Will your dog be allowed the food he normally eats? How many times a day will he have a run? Which vet do they use? Should you get your dog vaccinated for kennel cough? (Check this out with your own vet as well.) Do they have specific collection times? How many dogs do they have at once? How many staff?

Be suspicious of vague or incomplete answers: the owner of a well run kennel will have all this information at his fingertips. You will not enjoy yourself on holiday if you are worrying about your dog. If possible, before you go away, organize a trial night for your dog at the kennels – this will help you both.

If you don't want to leave your dog in kennels, a house sitter is another option. You could pay a friend who knows your dog. Alternatively, you could get a professional dog sitter, but check their references first. This is relatively expensive, but there is an advantage: your dog's routine will remain unaltered. If your dog is attending a training school, take your house sitter there for a session before you go, so he understands what's involved.

FIRST VISIT TO THE VET

Take treats. A young pup should not be allowed to develop a fear of the vet. Act confidently: it will rub off on your pup. The vet will fuss over him while doing the checks, but you still need to keep focused on your puppy.

The vet will probably want to put your dog on a table. Practise this at home, on a table that is not slippery.

When the vet gives a vaccination, distract your pup with a treat. Make sure the vet stamps your vaccination card, and keep it safe (you will need it for training school, or if your dog goes into kennels). Remember that vaccinations need to be updated annually. Worming and flea treatments should be repeated every three months. It is best to get these from the vet: the ones on sale in pet shops are usually not full strength and your vet will know which are right for your breed of dog.

It is essential to bring treats and toys with you on your first few visits to the vet.

FINDING THE RIGHT TRAINING SCHOOL

BASICS

Don't enrol at a training school that does not ask to see your dog's current vaccination certificate. If a school is relaxed about this, they may well be relaxed about other aspects of their work. Besides, at training school your dog will come into contact with dogs, and however charming their owners might be, you won't know where their dogs might have been.

To find a good school, word of mouth is always best. By all means search the internet and browse through advertisements in local newspapers, but when you find a training school that appeals to you, check it out by finding

From an early age, even in a class full of other dogs and handlers, your puppy will recognise you.

someone who has used it and asking them about their experiences. It really is worth the trouble.

Once you've narrowed down the search, ask the school if you can drop by in order to watch their training methods.

Take note of the floor. Some dog training schools have slippery floors. Although this may be beyond anyone's control, it may well be off-putting for a dog.

Ask the following basic questions. Do they have their own dogs present during training? If so, can they really concentrate on your dog? How do they discipline dogs? If they use harsh physical punishments or shout at the dogs, then avoid. Training is not a chore. It should be fun, a time for you and your dog to bond with each other and enjoy learning together: you don't want your dog to become traumatised.

How have the trainers gained their expertise? Some dog behaviourists, as they call themselves, have done nothing more than a correspondence course. They may only have trained their own dog, but still want to charge serious money for their services. If you get evasive answers, ask the questions again until you are satisfied. An experienced trainer or behaviourist should have an understanding of breeds and their specific traits, and be comfortable anwering any questions you may have.

Prepare your pup for adulthood by giving him a stimulating upbringing with varied activities. Always be consistent with your commands.

KEEPING AN EYE ON PROGRESS

The training school will probably see your dog for an hour a week. If your dog is well behaved in class, but not at home, then make this clear to the trainers. If you are not happy with progress, say so without delay. This way, there's a better chance the situation can be rectified by immediate action.

THE BEST AGE TO BEGIN AT TRAINING SCHOOL

Take a pup for socialisation classes as soon as he has been vaccinated. If you have taken on a rescue dog, start as you mean to go on. Book in to a class preferably within a couple of weeks. You and your dog will be learning to read each other's body language, and training will speed up this process. Puppy classes are fun, although sometimes hard work: other puppies can cause many distractions. Some think they are at a night club, rather than night school. But the socialization gained in this environment is invaluable.

Interacting with other handlers – and their puppies – at training school can be the making of well-socialised adult dogs.

WOULD MY DOG BE GOOD AT 'AGILITY' EXERCISES?

Jumping, running through tunnels and climbing is good fun for both handler and dog. Any breed of dog can enjoy this sport, provided the dog is fit, under reasonable control and capable of basic obedience training. The more obedience training you have done, the better your bond with your dog, and the easier the agility exercises will be.

Agility is done off the leash, so you want your dog to pay attention to you and not run after other dogs. Body language is extremely important here: your dog will constantly be looking to you to find out which way he has to go, and it is your body language that will show him. Whichever way you are facing, your dog will assume that that is the way forward. This is not difficult with a little practice.

Agility can be done for fun or competitively, and many a handler has started with no intention of entering competitions, but has enjoyed it so much that competitions become a major interest.

The tunnel is one of a dog's favourite obstacles.

The A-Frame. Agility is usually practised outside, so be prepared to train in all weather.

Agility exercises help burn off energy, and can work wonders for a rescue dog.

Mini dogs enjoy agility as much as they do sitting on your lap.

FLYBALL

This activity covers all the Fs in dog training: it's fast, furious and fun. Your dog jumps four small jumps, runs to a Flyball Box and presses the pad. The ball flies into the air, your dog catches it and comes racing back over the jumps to you. This is done in teams and creates much excitement, especially when teams compete against each other. It's noisy, and is mainly dominated by Collies because of their speed and endurance.

Other breeds can do well at Flyball, too, but it's obviously a game for a fast dog. After the initial training, you just stand there while your dog does the running.

Flyball hurdles are designed so that your dog can jump at speed and with ease.

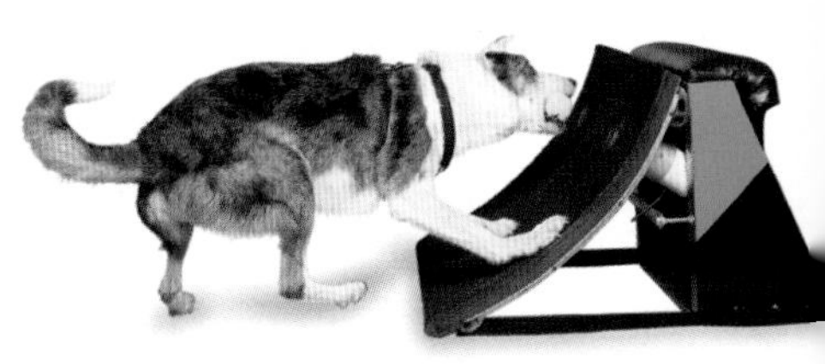

The dog leaps on to the machine to release the ball.

The home run, ball firmly held in the dog's mouth.

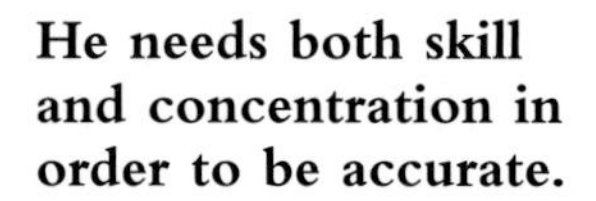

He needs both skill and concentration in order to be accurate.

HEEL WORK TO MUSIC

This is becoming more and more popular, and any dog and handler can do it. Essentially, it's all the tricks and exercises you have taught your dog put into a dance form. Treats and toys have to be used intensively in order to get your dog motivated. There are now worldwide heel work to music competitions, with wide variations in both music and style.

SPECIALIST TRAINING SCHOOLS

To find a school specializing in obedience, agility or flyball, follow the same basic steps outlined on page 178 for finding a basic obedience training school. Again, word of mouth is best; or your vet may have a list.

You should find that you are made welcome at training school, regardless of the breed of dog you own. Dog owners are some of the friendliest people about: after all, you have a common interest.

Small dogs often excel at heel work to music.

See how the dog reacts to the handler's body language, while moving naturally in time to the music.

HOW DO I GET MY DOG ON TV?

As well as my dog training school, I run a sister company that supplies dogs for films, TV and commercials. I get many enquiries from people who want their dog to be a film star. They say how gorgeous he is, and that he is quite well behaved...most of the time. This is very nice, but sadly not what I need to hear.

To stand any chance in the media world your dog needs to have an excellent temperament and behave perfectly for hours on end. A dog that does not stay or respond immediately to a command simply gets asked to leave the set. In the studio, time is money and expectations are high. The dog has to be used to noise, dozens of people, and being handled by strangers. You could simulate a TV studio by taking your dog to a hairdresser's shop, and doing some training there. There will be noise, wiring on the floor, bright lights. In fact, and I'm not joking, some hairdressers will actually oblige if you ask in the right way.

Clear hand signals and facial expressions become not just a good idea but a necessity. You can't call "Stay" to a dog while an actor is saying his lines. Any kind of dog can, potentially, get work, and looks aren't everything. It depends entirely what the director needs.

The hours are long and there is plenty of waiting about. It is not glamorous work and can be very tiring, but the dogs have a great time, are well cared for and have plenty of play and rest – far more than the handlers. Often, the day starts early after a long journey, and ends late in the evening. Times and dates are constantly changed at the last minute: you have to be flexible. You may be out for 16 hours and see your dog on screen for two seconds: but it is very rewarding to achieve even this and it's lovely to see your dog on TV or in a catalogue. The results still give me a feeling of pride.

Your first move should be to look on the internet or in a directory of animal agents. Send them photos of your dog, and don't be disappointed if you hear nothing: it's highly competitive. But you could just get lucky, and it's worth

The first audition.

making sure that the photos you send are the best. Take a head shot and a full body shot – playing with a toy is fine. Make the background simple, and don't slide yourself into the picture, however cute you are. Nothing should distract from your dog. Photos taken in a field are usually successful: green grass highlights a dog of any colour.

VINNIE'S FIRST ROLE

My introduction to the film and TV industry was through an agency. I was asked to supply a black Labrador for a TV series, and the most suitable dog I had at the time was a lovely animal called Vinnie. I was so looking forward to my first TV job that even getting up at 4 am didn't seem to matter.

After a couple of hours on the road we arrived at the location. I tried to look cool, not too much like a star-struck fan. All the dog had to do was sit by a door and bark on command as the actor came through the door. The director even allowed Vinnie's name to be used. The command had to be a signal, and the only place where I could put myself so as not to appear in the shot was in a flowerbed. I had to stay low and give a hand signal to Vinnie when the director gave me mine.

Fortunately, Vinnie was brilliant and after about the sixth take he even knew when to bark without a signal. By then I had cramp, and had lost sensation in both my legs. I was surprised at how many times they repeated takes, and from how many different angles, but Vinnie had impressed the director so much that he asked us to stay and do another scene later that night. Vinnie had a great time: all the crew fed him and he had plenty of play. I eventually got home at 1.30 in the morning, but I was thoroughly hooked and wanted to learn more about the TV and film business. The satisfaction of seeing Vinnie on screen, even for less than a minute, made it all hugely worthwhile.

SOAP

After that, I supplied dogs for several other TV dramas and films, and this led to my setting up my own agency. The first contract was a major soap, and the dog I supplied was Ebony, the Brindle Boxer. The lead actor was superb with Ebony, and they formed a great bond, which was a delight to watch. Ebony was a dream to work with, and became known as the one-take dog. I wondered sometimes if her owner and I were needed. All the cast and crew loved her, and we were even allowed in the Green Room.

In one scene, Ebony had to be carried in by an actor and laid down on a table. She had to lie very still while the actors said their lines. I was standing just behind the director, ready to help if needed. In came Ebony; down she went on to the table; I gave a 'stay' hand signal and watched. Silence. As usual, Ebony was one hundred per cent obedient. Then, when the dialogue was just about to start, Ebony broke wind. Loud and smelly.

Everyone burst into laughter, except the one actor who was in the firing line. The director shouted "Cut", the crew fanned away the smell with sheets of paper and the director shouted "We'll go

again." Ebony had not moved a muscle and got a round of applause.

It was a sad day when they axed the series. The cast and crew were like a family, but I have been lucky enough to work with some of them again.

Basset Hounds are popular for roles in soap operas, comedies and with advertising moguls, due to their lovely long ears and comical/sad expressions.

THE THINGS PEOPLE SAY/1

MEMORABLE QUOTES FROM MY TRAINING SCHOOL

"He does it right at home."

Do your training wherever you walk your dog – not just at home. This way he will perform at school.

"I'm not praising him, because he gets excited."

He must learn that if he goes over the top, the praise stops. Praise gently.

"I took him out before he came, I just don't know where all that came from."

Make sure your dog has time to empty his bowels and bladder before attending training school.

"It's OK, he won't bite!"

If you are not in charge, he may feel he has to protect you. Make sure you are in full control of your dog at all times.

"He only wants to play. He won't bite your dog."

Be careful: two young dogs might feel the need to dominate each other.

"He's distracted by the other dogs."

In the big, wide world there are many distractions. See pages 144–145 for how to cope with these.

THE THINGS PEOPLE SAY/2

MEMORABLE QUOTES FROM MY TRAINING SCHOOL

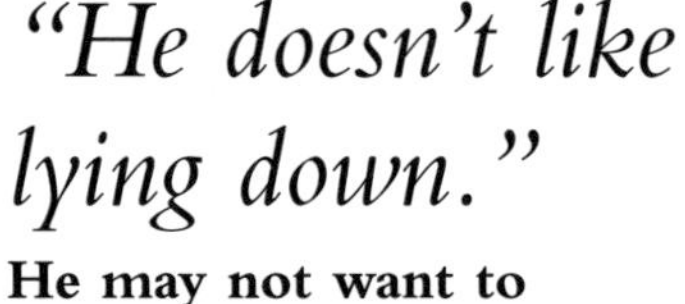

"He doesn't like lying down."

He may not want to appear submissive in a room full of dogs.

"He can shake a paw."

This is not so good if he scratches your legs.

"Sorry, I couldn't hear you, my dog was barking."

Use a treat or a toy to divert his attention.

"Will you sit down now? Sit. Sit. Sit. Sit. Oh. Forget it."

Just look at the handler's incorrect body language. **See pages 56-57.**

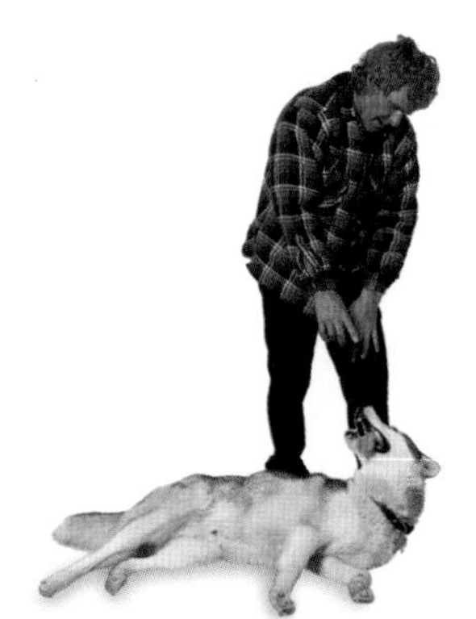

"I'm sure he'll embarrass me."

There is nothing your dog could do that a trainer has not seen before.

"He's never done that before, but he is greedy."

The handler has not noticed that his dog is pinching treats off the handler next to him. Training should educate him not to behave like this, but still watch what your dog is doing – at all times.

TALES FROM A DOG TRAINING SCHOOL

Stories for when you are not training your dog.

MOLLY AND BEN

Some years ago, before I got hold of a building specifically for my training school, I had to hire different venues. One of these was a dilapidated riding school. There were gaping holes in the roof, pigeons on the rafters and rats scurrying around. Owners of horses would come in and dump stable muck. As the building was large, we would often get out the jumps and send the dogs over four in a row: a difficult exercise, and many a dog would have a great time just running around the large arena instead of keeping to the jumps.

A large gentleman turned up one day with a whippet-type crossbreed called Molly. I shall call him Ben. To Ben's dismay, when Molly tried the jumps for the first time she did three, but ran around the fourth. However, this was a good effort compared with the previous attempts.

Molly wasn't alone: every other dog failed at the last hurdle. Then it came to Molly's turn once more. Unlike the handlers who made their dogs sit, then gave a command and waited to see what happened, Ben made Molly sit, then bent down over her and laboriously explained step by step exactly what to do: "Molly, now you go and jump the first jump; then run to the next one and jump that; then to the next one and jump that. And don't you go round the last one like the others. You go and jump it, and then you go and lie down. Be a good girl Molly."

He had a speech impediment so it was very difficult for us to understand him – let alone for an animal. We were all convinced that Molly would have forgotten what to do by the time she was able to go. When Molly's turn came, Ben stood up, unclipped her leash and just sort of grunted.

Molly tore off, did all of the jumps perfectly, then dropped into the 'down' and looked at him. Ben was ecstatic, jumping up and down shouting "She done it, she done it, good girl".

Some bitches get temperamental during their season, and will squabble with each other. This can lead to serious fights.

I learnt a lot from Ben. He had such a lovely bond with his dog, and she had adapted to his awkward way of speaking, and understood him as no one else could. He worked his way with Molly up through all our classes, ending in the top class and the display team. Every time he got something right, we all knew about it: he jumped up and down and shouted. The partnership between Ben and Molly would often bring a tear to the eye.

To see the bo between handler and dog is always special. Here, both are showing that their body language has almost merged together – an example of rea teamwork.

JIMBOB THE SPRINGER

All breeds have their peculiarities. Even when thoroughly domesticated, the natural instinct of the breed often shows through. For example: Border Collies need to round up people and animals; Rottweilers guard the pack; Springer Spaniels use their noses – which brings me to the next tale.

After completing several obedience courses, handlers and their dogs at my school take a test: passing it is a real achievement, and is rewarded with a certificate, presented at the annual get-together. A lady with a Springer named Jimbob had worked extremely hard, doing more than the usual number of courses before feeling that she was ready for the test.

Jimbob, a very happy-go-lucky lad, with a tail that could spin for England, had worked brilliantly for weeks, but on the day of the test his owner was still nervous. We were out of doors, in a large field, and she was worried he might get distracted. The heel work, on and off the leash, went very well and she only lost a point when Jimbob sat crooked. He was perfect on the 'Stays' and did a good recall. He even ignored a bird in the distance when he did his 'Retrieve'.

The final exercise was the 'Sendaway'. This involved sending the dog away from the handler in a straight line and then dropping him on command into the 'Down'. Not easy. Everyone was worried about this exercise, and several of the dogs only went a short distance.

Jimbob's owner had told me this one worried her the most. The night before, at practice, he had refused to lie down when commanded from a distance. As she lined Jimbob up, you could hear a pin drop. "Away," she ordered, and off shot Jimbob in a fast, but straight line. It looked good. Only one dog had completed the exercise properly so far.

But just as he was about to reach the spot where he was supposed to lie down, he suddenly veered off to the left. Without a thought of slowing down, he just kept going. His owner was shouting "Down", "Stay", "Come" and "Jimbob" but with zero effect.

Spaniels' noses are designed for scenting. This is why they are frequently used as drug search dogs.

We watched him disappear across the field, down the bank, through the river and, with sinking hearts, into the sewage farm. He could really move, and his tail was spinning all the time. His owner took off in hot pursuit.

Half an hour later they were back. Jimbob had changed from a lovely liver-and-white, silky, shiny-coated Springer into a slimy, walking manure heap. His tongue was nearly on the floor, but the tail, of course, was still spinning at the sight of his friends. When his owner had recovered enough to talk, she explained that he had been in the sewage pools, but that he did come and sit perfectly straight in front of her when she arrived. She looked down at him, oblivious to everyone, and said: "Well Jimbob, you have had a good day." Then she turned to the judge and said: "I suppose he failed."

The next test day, several months later, Jimbob passed with flying colours, but the test was done in an enclosed tennis court.

LUGER

My late German Shepherd, Luger, was a star at charity events where we put on displays. He would chase a 'criminal', stopping him in his tracks by grabbing an arm in his mouth, then releasing the arm on command and detaining him by barking. I would then run up, clip the leash on the dog and frog march the criminal out of the arena to the crowd's applause. It worked every time.

Luger loved this routine and treated it as a game. He would get very excited and his grip on the arm, (covered as a precaution by a thick leather sleeve), could be very tight indeed. The criminal was one of our trainers, who got on very well with Luger until he put on his balaclava and started running.

On one occasion I noticed that the trainer had put the sleeve on the wrong arm. I called out to Luger, who obediently stopped and dropped into the 'down'. You could hear the laughter from the audience and you could see the embarassment on the trainer's face. I called Luger back and set him up again, but now he was agitated because he had missed his game of tugging on the sleeve.

Once again, the trainer appeared in his balaclava and started running. Again, Luger was in full flight. But this time, the sleeve shot off the trainer's arm. Luger, the trainer and I froze. Luger almost had his teeth into the criminal's arm when he leapt the 5-foot fence. I called to Luger who again stopped, turned round, grabbed the sleeve from the ground and gave it a good ragging, much to the audience's delight.

SALLY THE SLAPPER

A new dog in my training school always creates added excitement, but none so much as Sally, a lovely blond Retriever bitch. The animals already in training were mainly young adolescent dogs, so hormones were running high.

As the dogs were introduced to Sally, I noticed that some of them were reluctant to leave her, and even got grumpy with each other: unusual, since they normally got on well. Sally was in her element, wagging her tail at them all, and quickly earned the nickname Sally the Slapper.

The dogs in this group had done very well with their training, but you would have thought that night was the first for most of them. They were very unsettled in the 'stays' and all the recalls had to be done on the leash.

As it was Sally's owner's first night, I was embarrassed by how poorly the dogs performed, and worried that she should be unimpressed with the school. Sally, however, responded well. In fact, she did better than several of the adolescent dogs who had been in training for weeks. As it had been a hot day, and by now the air was warm and muggy, I thought perhaps that a storm was on the way, and that this was making the dogs nervous. One handler with a very lively labrador announced that her dog got anxious when thunder was brewing, and that he could certainly sense it.

By the end of the class the dogs had just started to respond, with help from extra treats. As Sally's owner was leaving the car park, she wound down her window and said "Thank you." "I didn't think Sally would do so well; I nearly didn't bring her tonight, because I thought she would be naughty and not be able to concentrate in a group of dogs." Still not realising the truth, I smiled and replied: "Well, she did very well, she is so lovely and friendly." "Yes she is", came the reply. "But apparently some dogs can be very grumpy when they're around a bitch in season. Bye". And off she drove.

I spent the next day disinfecting and hosing down the school in order to get rid of Sally's scent. And I did ring Sally's owner to explain (in depth) that while Sally was in season, she wasn't welcome at training classes. Sally was this woman's first dog and she hadn't had time to read the rules on her membership card. They both returned once Sally's season was over and settled nicely. But Sally's nickname stayed with her.

SEBASTIAN THE POODLE

Running a dog training school means meeting all sorts of people, and all sorts of dogs. The majority of them are charming. One thing all the owners have in common is their love of their dogs. And another – they don't always understand them.

One particular lady springs to mind. She was always immaculately dressed and very well spoken, but her knowledge of dogs was limited. Her animal was a young, standard Poodle named Sebastian, and his manners weren't as good as hers.

Sebastian's owner adored him, though he clearly pushed her to the limit on several occasions. One Christmas, she left him in the kitchen for a few minutes while she went to greet her family, who were arriving for lunch. Fortunately, for her, they all liked dogs: just as well, because while her back was turned, naughty Sebastian dragged the freshly-cooked turkey off the work surface and into the garden.

After cold ham with all the trimmings, the family settled

down for a restful afternoon, marred only by Sebastian's flatulence. (Turkey is too rich for a dog and all too often has this effect.) He also threw up on the carpet.

Sebastian's first trip to the groomers didn't go as planned: he was so naughty that they refused to book him in for another session. When he got home, he went straight into the garden and rolled on something rather pungent in the flower bed. It was after this that Sebastian came to my training school.

I had a long chat with his owner about his behaviour and she agreed that she had been spoiling him, but was now determined to have a well-behaved dog. She explained that as a child she had always wanted a Poodle because they looked so glamorous. The problem with Sebastian, she said, was that he just didn't 'do' glamour. He was only six months old when he had turned the whole house upside down, "And", she whispered, "he even eats the cat's poo."

To be fair to Sebastian, he was very intelligent and took to training. His owner changed her lovely white trousers for brown cords and wellies, and took control. Soon he was even well behaved at his new groomers. He no longer pinched food or ate cat poo (a delicacy for a dog). The command "Leave" was used frequently.

While we were practising 'stays' one evening, Sebastian decided to take the opportunity to do some very personal grooming. Again, his owner was whispering to me, clearly very embarrassed: "Why does he do that?"
I really couldn't help myself. "Because he can" was all I could say. For a moment, everyone was silent, then she collapsed laughing. "Well that's Sebastian, isn't it?" she giggled.

They continued with their training for several courses

A great comfort and companion.

and even got some rosettes at a local show. When I last spoke to her, she was considering getting a second dog as a playmate for Sebastian – a bitch, of course, because even this soft-hearted lady knew that one Sebastian was enough for a family.

INDEX

ACKNOWLEDGMENTS & THANKS

The author and editors would like to thank the following for additional photography: Shutterstock: 63, 66, 82, 107; Interpet: 71, 93, 101, 117; Dorling Kindersley:135, 127.

Su would also like to offer her personal thanks and appreciation to the following:

Firstly, to photographer, Bill Stephenson, for urging me to write this book, and for his patience and understanding during the shoots. And of course, special thanks to all the pupils (and dogs) featured in the book, and to the trainers, Colin Arthur (Flyn and Barley); Margaret Moores (Domino); Paul Madeley (Roxy and Prince); Phil and Jaqui Lees (Barney and Gizmo); Heather Gordon (Hamish); Gary Dutton (Monkey and Tinker); Nichola Riley (Sophie); Samantha Brown (Jola); Ian Millward (Tsar and Reece); not only for their immense help, but for being excellent models and having such well-behaved dogs during photography. Thanks to Jane Redican (Rodrey), for make up and wardrobe assistance; Fiona Martin (Ada), for modelling and assisting with the shoots; Samantha Arthur for being an excellent model and a pleasure to work with; Colin and Sam and their two young children, Connor and Jersey; Margaret Moores, an extra thank you for your support and help while writing; Mandy Cain (Rye and Jess) for the supply of Flyball equipment; Terry and Shirley Heath (Bracken and Shap) for the use of their farm and cattle; Pearl and David Stonier (Bertie), for allowing us to use their home for a photoshoot; and Kevin Fairclough for his much-needed computer advice and support.

Thanks to my mother Glenise, brother Alan (Genna), and nephew Elliot (Millie), for their support and for travelling the distance. And last, but not least, thanks to my dogs Soni, Gal and to Roger the cat.